TOWARDS A FULLER LIFE IN THE HOLY SPIRIT

Many blessings,

Charles

First published in 2011 by
New Life Publishing, Luton,
Bedfordshire LU4 9HG
with additions in 2014

British Library Cataloguing in Publication Data
A catalogue record for this book is available
from the British Library

ISBN   978 1 912237 07 4

Typesetting by New Life Publishing,
Luton, UK www.goodnewsbooks.net
Printed and bound in Great Britain

TOWARDS A FULLER LIFE IN THE HOLY SPIRIT

SCRIPTURAL REFLECTIONS ON
THE PERSON OF THE HOLY SPIRIT
AND HIS WORK IN OUR LIVES

CHARLES WHITEHEAD

NEW LIFE PUBLISHING

*To Sue with gratitude and love -
my wife, greatest supporter,
faithful companion on
life's exciting journey,
and my best friend*

COMMENDATIONS

Charles Whitehead, the quintessential English Catholic, is a remarkably gifted leader, speaker, and ecumenist. These qualities are evident in his latest book on the nature, role, fruits, and gifts of the Holy Spirit. Like good wine, its contents have been fermenting in the vats of his mind and heart for a long time. Clearly, it is based on prayerful reflection on scripture, informed by many years of pastoral experience, and expressed in a lucid and practical way. I am confident that, not only will this gem of a book be widely used for private devotion and as a teaching aid, in all likelihood it is destined to become a classic of Charismatic spirituality.

Fr. Pat Collins, Congregation of the Mission

In *Towards a Fuller Life in the Holy Spirit*, Charles Whitehead explains why the experience of the Holy Spirit is so crucial in the Christian life. Drawing from the Bible, Charles writes about the person and work of the Holy Spirit in a way that is accessible to everyone.

Revd. Nicky Gumbel, Vicar of Holy Trinity Brompton

Charles Whitehead provides a truly excellent explanation of why the contemporary interest in the Holy Spirit isn't a passing fad or an optional extra, but an absolutely essential feature of what it means to live as a Christian today. There are few men I admire more than Charles in his steadfast service in helping so many discover what it really means to live a Spirit-filled life as faithful Church members. Highly recommended.
Dr. Ralph Martin, Renewal Ministries

I have been honoured to call Charles Whitehead my friend for over thirty years because I see the life of Jesus in him. Although our churchmanship and spiritual journeys have differed our desires have always been to fulfil God's purposes; honour Jesus as Lord and Saviour; maintain an openness of life to the person and ministry of the Holy Spirit; acknowledge the authority of Scripture; and be eager to see the Kingdom of God breaking out of eternity into history. *Towards a Fuller Life in the Holy Spirit* embraces all of these things with practicality, clarity and integrity.

Clearly it is written for Catholics, yet it is unmistakably helpful for all of us of other Denominational convictions. This book is a 'must' for personal renewal (I had a new encounter with the Holy Spirit during the days I set apart to read it and reflect upon it slowly!) It also gives an excellent framework for Small Group or congregational teaching and study. In these challenging days when many of our hearts are crying to God, "Restore, O Lord, the honour of Your Name; in works of sovereign power come shake the earth again" both inside and outside the Church, Charles' book makes a significant, relevant and timely contribution.
Revd. Jim Graham, Pastor Emeritus at Gold Hill Baptist Church

The clarity and precision that is the hallmark of Charles Whitehead's writing, has produced *Towards a Fuller Life in the Holy Spirit*. It is a comprehensive guide to the person, work, power, gifts, and fruit of the Holy Spirit. It is scripturally based, theologically solid, historically accurate, and filled with the wisdom of years spent living and teaching the life of the Spirit. Whether used in bible study, Confirmation preparation, or as inspiration for those who seek more of the Lord, I highly recommend this book. ***Dorothy Garrity Ranaghan, a leader in the People of Praise Covenant Community***

Charles Whitehead has a remarkable gift for clear and direct teaching that goes to the heart of things. This book is no popularization at the expense of the depths and riches of the biblical revelation. It opens up the deep workings of the Holy Spirit revealed in the Scriptures in practical and accessible ways. Charles' pithy summaries are brilliant, capturing all aspects of his topic in punchy phrases. This book will bring much blessing to all who are open to the 'more' that the Lord has for all of us. ***Monsignor Peter Hocken, Diocese of Northampton***

CONTENTS

FOREWORD

Charles Whitehead has been one of the most influential Catholic lay men of the era since the Second Vatican Council. For eleven years he was President of the International Council for Catholic Charismatic Renewal. In that capacity he worked closely with the Pontifical Council for the Laity and met frequently with Pope John Paul II. One of the outstanding features of the papacy of Blessed John Paul was the growth of new movements and communities in the Church which he saw as a fruit of the Council. Although the Charismatic Renewal is not a movement as such, many new communities have been inspired by it and are part of it. It was significant that at a gathering of new movements and communities in Rome on the eve of Pentecost, 1998, Charles Whitehead was invited to respond to the Pope's address on behalf of them all.

It is with that background and in the light of that experience that Charles Whitehead has written *Towards a Fuller Life in the Holy Spirit*. It will soon become clear to the reader, however, that this book also finds roots in the whole Pentecostal revival of the twentieth century. This is a book, therefore, that is genuinely ecumenical. Moreover it is clear throughout that its deepest roots are in the Scriptures and especially in the teaching of St Paul on the gifts of the Holy Spirit.

This book is not intended to be a comprehensive and finely-balanced exposition of the theology of the Holy Spirit. Rather, it is a plea for Christians to expect and pray for the gifts of the Holy Spirit. Charles Whitehead reminds us that over 120 million Catholics have come to deeper faith through the Renewal and that in Christianity generally this is overwhelmingly the fastest area of growth. That is why this book is timely. In it the author explains clearly what is meant by the Baptism in the Holy Spirit and explores all the issues relating to the gifts of the Holy Spirit. He writes with passion, conviction and authority. Most importantly, Charles Whitehead is not proposing any great new programme or agenda for the Church or for Christians generally. His book is simply an encouragement to be open to the gifts that God has given us in Jesus Christ.

+Kevin McDonald
Archbishop Emeritus of Southwark

INTRODUCTION

Many people are questioning whether this new emphasis on the importance of the Holy Spirit is just another religious fad that will fade away like many before it, whether its proponents are eccentric people, a group of campaigning enthusiasts, and if the Spirit really has an important part to play in the way we live our lives as Christians today. They quite reasonably want to know why, if this focus on the person and work of the Spirit is so essential, they heard little about it before. It's a good question. I hope that these pages will help to answer it.

What follows was first written in 1979, but it is only now that I have decided to update, edit and publish it. My original reasons for writing it were straightforward – in spite of receiving one of the best Catholic educations available, I had drifted away from the Church during my university years and only found my way back in 1976. By that time I was 34 years old, happily married to Sue, our first two children Lucy and Adam were 8 and 7, and I was following a promising career in the papermaking and marketing industry. But I knew something was missing; why had I drifted from the Church? After all, the Jesuits had done a good job teaching me theology, doctrine, and apologetics, but I found these of little help in my day-to-day life. The answer I discovered was simple. I had completely failed to grasp the basic fact that the Holy Spirit, present in me through my Baptism and Confirmation, would bring me the power I needed to live an active and effective Christian life

- but he needed my co-operation. Without it, the effects of the grace received were bound to be limited. Until I understood this, and allowed the Spirit freedom to work in and through me, it was always going to be an uphill struggle – one which I had very little chance of winning.

The comparison that comes to mind is pushing my car along the road because no one has told me there is fuel in the tank, and all I need to do is turn the ignition key and start the engine. We are not supposed to live the Christian life without the power of the Holy Spirit - why else would Jesus tell his disciples to wait in Jerusalem until they received the 'power from on high', after which they were to take his message of love, new life, and salvation throughout the world? On Pentecost Day, we read that they were all 'filled with the Holy Spirit' and they immediately set about doing exactly what Jesus had said they were to do. They realised that the Spirit had come to empower them and that if they co-operated with him, then anything and everything was possible. An in-filling with the Holy Spirit should always be followed by an out-flowing, a reaching out to others with the Gospel message in word and deed.

It was this same simple fact that Sue and I discovered in 1976 through the remarkable witness of a small group of Christians from different local churches – Anglican, Baptist, and Catholic. How had I missed this central truth of the Christian faith, why had no one pointed it out to me before? As a baptised and confirmed Catholic, the issue was not had I got the Holy Spirit – of course I had. The real question was, had the Holy Spirit got me? And the answer to that was quite clear – no, he had not. Once I realised this and deliberately surrendered my life to Jesus and his Holy Spirit, it was as if someone had started my spiritual engine and I was off. Life would never be quite the same again. I had given the power, which I had usurped, back to God. I had learned that *"the God of Israel gives power and strength to his people" Psalm 68:35*, and that this power and strength comes through the Holy Spirit.

We all start our spiritual journeys not really knowing who we are, what we've got, what is available to us, or exactly where we're going. It's the Holy Spirit who reveals all this – if we ask him to. From that moment of revelation it has been a wonderful, exciting, challenging, and fulfilling journey for us, and for that I am so grateful to God, to that small ecumenical group who showed us a living faith, and to the many remarkable people we have met along the way. Although we had no idea what the years ahead had in store for us, Sue and I realised in 1976 that a great adventure was beginning, and we wanted to give others the key that would start their spiritual engines too. So **'Towards a Fuller Life in the Holy Spirit'** was born in 1979, and as I look around me now, I realise that the need to understand the person and work of the Holy Spirit in our lives is even greater today than it was then – things haven't changed for the better. We live in a precarious world, and if ever there was a need for Christians living in the fullness of the power of the Holy Spirit, it is in our nations today. We need spiritual renewal.

One of the challenges I've faced in writing this short book is how to maintain a correct balance between theology and experience. God created us with emotions as well as minds, but our demands to understand everything, even the deepest mysteries of God, and to be able to explain it all in a rationally enlightened way, can mean we miss out on God's supernatural activity. We often suppress the emotional and experiential side of our nature because we don't want to appear naïve and foolish. Of course we must be adult about our faith, but Jesus expects us to be child-like in our approach to the divine mysteries, often accepting things we do not fully understand: *"unless you change and become like little children, you will never enter the kingdom of heaven" Matthew 18:2.* Little children are trusting, and usually more concerned with how they feel about things than with what they understand. As adults we need to hold these two things in balance, rather than adopting an attitude of intellectual superiority and dismissing our emotions as childish signs of immaturity.

I usually teach by including stories in what I say or write. The reason for this is that a true story, based on someone's personal experience, often my own, challenges disinterest and intellectual superiority, whilst reinforcing the spiritual message I want to convey. This was how Jesus often taught his disciples and the crowds that came to listen to him. But instead of including stories in **'Towards a Fuller Life in the Holy Spirit'**, I've taken the decision to rely on the Scriptures to challenge any sceptics.

After all, *"...the word of God is living and active. Sharper than any double-edged sword, it penetrates even to dividing soul and spirit, joints and marrow; it judges the thoughts and attitudes of the heart. Nothing in all creation is hidden from God's sight. Everything is uncovered and laid bare before the eyes of him to whom we must give account." Hebrews 4:12-13.*

I've learned that God can speak for himself - we don't have to defend him, only proclaim him. Catholics, for whom this is mainly but not exclusively written, are not for the most part people of the Word. This in spite of the fact that Catholic teaching is rooted in the

Scriptures, demonstrated by the fact that every document of the Church is full of references to the Word of God, and that we hear three or four Scriptures proclaimed every time we gather to celebrate Eucharist together. My own love for the Scriptures makes me confident that they can challenge and convict both the heart and mind of every reader of this book, as they reveal the person and work of the Holy Spirit in amazing new ways: *"Your Word is a lamp to my feet and a light for my path" Psalm 119:105.* If I am correct in this, it follows that there is little need here for anecdotes and personal illustrations.

Other reasons for deciding to take a scriptural approach to my topic are that all Christians share and respect the Scriptures, and that in 1976 I fell in love with the Word of God – a love which is just as strong today as it was then. In Catholic understanding, God's revelation comes to us through the Scriptures and Tradition, the twin foundations on which the teaching of the Church is based. The Scriptures are the account of God's relationship with his people since he created the world, reaching a climax in the mission of his son, Jesus Christ, and including the fascinating story of the early years in the lives of the first Christian communities. The Bible is not just one book – it's a library of life-changing books written by human authors using their natural abilities, but inspired and guided by the Holy Spirit. What we know as the Old and New Testaments were brought together by scholars of the early church in a place called Biblius in the Lebanon – hence the name Bible used to describe the Scriptures.

Tradition, for its part, is the lived experience of the members of the Christian community since the time of Jesus, based on their reflections on the Scriptures and the teaching of the Apostles, and

handed down to us through successive generations of bishops of
the Church - the successors of the Apostles. All this accumulated
wisdom is penetrated and interpreted through the teaching
authority vested in the bishops, the Magisterium, watched over and
guided by the Holy Spirit. This authority is not superior to the
Word of God, but is its servant - it exists to protect the Scriptures
from erroneous interpretation and to ensure correct teaching. All
the preaching of the Church is to be ruled by the sacred Scriptures
and Tradition, so it is on the written Word of God and the teaching
of the Apostles and their successors that our faith rests today. By
focusing these reflections on a scriptural presentation of the person
and work of the Holy Spirit, my hope is that not only will they be
accessible to everyone – all you need is a Bible, a notebook and a
little time – but also easy to follow and understand. Whilst the Bible
is always accessible, we do of course have to pick it up and read it,
so since 1976 I have built into my busy life a habit of daily reading
of the Scriptures. In these pages I will, therefore, be quoting the
Scriptures more than any other sources to show what they reveal
to us about the Holy Spirit.

The translation of the Scriptures I am using, unless otherwise
stated, is the New International Version © 1973, International Bible
Society, and I do so because more and more people from all
denominations are using this scholarly but user-friendly text. I will
also refer to the new Catechism of the Catholic Church containing
today's complete Catholic teaching on faith, doctrine and morals,
and sometimes I'll make reference to one of the official documents
or encyclicals of the Church, or to the words of recent Popes as well
as quotations from the early Church Fathers and some prominent
Protestant writers. When our understanding of the Holy Spirit rests
on the promises of Scripture and on the teaching of the Church, we

can face anyone criticising us with confidence and assurance. In 1979 I decided to cover the teaching by answering a number of frequently asked questions about the Holy Spirit, as this helps to keep a focus on the main issues. Little has changed – I am still asked the same questions, and I still give the same answers. I try to do so in a very straightforward and uncomplicated way - I hope you find this to be true as you read **'Towards a Fuller Life in the Holy Spirit'.**

So here at last is this book, presented to you with the added benefit of whatever wisdom I have acquired over the years of walking the walk. I have tried to write in a way that is accessible to everyone, and this means I may have over-simplified some complex theological issues. It's quite short, and can be read like any other book, but the style and approach I have adopted is also that of a study guide, which has the advantage that it can also be used as an individual or group Scripture study on the person and work of the Holy Spirit. This is why each chapter concludes with some passages of Scripture and questions for discussion or personal reflection as appropriate.

My original foreword read as follows:
"The thoughts which are contained in the following pages were put together over a number of weeks as the basis for a series of teachings on the Holy Spirit given to our prayer group in Chalfont St. Peter. I make no claim to be anything more than an ordinary Christian to whom God has been gracious enough to reveal himself in a new and wonderful way through the ministry of the Holy Spirit. I owe a deep debt of gratitude to many Christian writers, teachers and preachers, whose ministries have contributed so much to what is contained in the following pages, and to the many people I have met since 1976 whose lives bear ample witness to

the work of the Holy Spirit in our midst. I submit the following pages in humility and love, praying that they may in some part be helpful in opening doors which are still closed, and allowing the Holy Spirit to enter and carry out his wonderful work in our lives."

What I wrote then is just as true today, many years later, and this simple resource is no more than an attempt to explain the one who is our amazing friend, helper and guide through life:

the Father-glorifying, Jesus-revealing, sin-exposing, joy-giving, love-imparting, relationship-building, holiness-encouraging, energy-releasing, truth-telling, witness-enabling, gift-bearing, miracle-working, fruit-producing, power-providing, life-changing – the incomparable and indispensable third Person of the Trinity, **God the Holy Spirit!**

Charles Whitehead

CHAPTER ONE

THE PERSON OF THE HOLY SPIRIT

- **Who is the Holy Spirit?**
- **Is there a clear distinction between the Father, Son, and Holy Spirit, and is the Holy Spirit as important as the Father and the Son?**
- **What is his Personality and what does he do?**
- **Are we giving too much emphasis to the Holy Spirit?**

WHO IS THE HOLY SPIRIT?

Many of us begin by thinking of the Spirit as an influence - intangible, present around us, perhaps producing a warm feeling, but somehow unreal. We used to call him the Holy Ghost, thereby contributing to an impression that he was not really a person, and supported this by often using the impersonal pronoun 'it' when referring to the Holy Ghost. This made it very unlikely we would visualise the Holy Spirit as a person.

The Father is clearer to us – artists portray him in human form and we are familiar with human fathers, so it is much easier to think of

him as a person. Jesus the Son is also clearly a person - in the
gospels we read of him living among ordinary people and doing
many of the normal things we do. We are surrounded by images of
him - every time we enter a Catholic church we see him hanging
on the cross. So most of us do not have difficulty with the persons
of the Father or the Son. But the Spirit? It's hard to recognise him
as a person because we have no image of him in human form.

Symbols of the Spirit

In the Bible he is described as **Wind, Fire, Cloud, Water, Oil,
Breath, Light** and at the baptism of Jesus he descends in the form
of a **Dove**, which is how he is usually depicted in religious art:

*"When all the people were being baptised, Jesus was baptised too.
And as he was praying, heaven was opened and the Holy Spirit
descended on him in bodily form like a dove" Luke 3:21-22.*

But even if none of the above Scriptural symbols help us to see the
Spirit as a person, it's important to take a brief look to see what
each may reveal about the attributes of the Holy Spirit.

Dove

The dove is a symbol of peace and of love, gentle, and free to fly
wherever it chooses - a good image for the Holy Spirit. After the
great flood, Noah releases a dove to fly over the waters *"to see if
the waters had receded from the surface of the ground" Genesis 8:8.*
This reminds us of the beginning of the creation story in *Gen.1:2
"...and the Spirit of God was hovering over the waters".*

Wind

Wind can be powerful, destroying and challenging, or gentle, light, enjoyable, refreshing - hardly noticeable. This reminds us that the Spirit comes to us in many different ways, including a mighty wind or a gentle breeze:

"The wind blows wherever it pleases. You hear its sound but you cannot tell where it comes from or where it is going. So it is with everyone born of the Spirit" John 3:8.

Fire

Fire suggests heat, energy, and power, or cleansing and destruction. The fire of the Spirit will cleanse and energise us. As John the Baptist said of Jesus:

"I baptise you with water for repentance. But after me will come one who is more powerful than I, whose sandals I am not fit to carry. He will baptise you with the Holy Spirit and with fire" Matthew 3:11.

Fire is a sign of God's presence – think of Moses and the Burning Bush, the Pillar of Fire, Elijah at Mount Carmel and the fire from heaven. The writer to the Hebrews reminds us: *"Our God is a consuming fire" Hebrews 12:29.*

Cloud

Clouds are mysterious, always moving – they hide things which are then suddenly revealed. They may be soft and gentle, or overshadowing and obscuring. As the **Catholic Catechism** explains it in section 697: *"the cloud, now obscure, now luminous, reveals the living and saving God, while veiling the transcendence of his glory".* This is true of Moses on Mount Sinai *(Ex.24:15-18)*; at the tent of meeting *(Ex.33:9-10)*; during wandering in the desert *(Ex.40:36-38)*, at the dedication of the Temple *(1 Kings 8:10-12)*. The

Spirit comes upon Mary and the power of the Most High overshadows her *(Lk.1:35)*; at the Transfiguration the cloud covers Jesus and the two disciples *(Lk.9:34-35)*; at his Ascension *(Acts 1:9)* a cloud hides Jesus until the time he will come again on a cloud with great glory *(Lk.21:27)*.

Water

Water is refreshing, cleansing, and life-giving - a place with no water is a desert. Water is essential for all life, and the Spirit is the water of our spiritual life:

"If anyone is thirsty, let him come to me and drink. Whoever believes in me, as the Scripture has said, streams of living water will flow from within him." By this he meant the Spirit, whom those who believed in him were later to receive John 7: 37-39.

Oil

We can cook with oil, produce light, and soothe our tired bodies with oil. In the Scriptures, oil is used for anointing, for consecration to God's service (reminding us of the sacraments), for healing, and for sealing. When Samuel goes to the house of Jesse to anoint David as the future King of Israel the Lord says: *"Rise and anoint him; he is the one"*, *1 Samuel 16:12*. Jesus himself declared: *"The Spirit of the Lord is on me, because he has anointed me..." Luke 4:18.* And Paul reminds us that: *"...you were marked in him with a seal – the promised Holy Spirit, who is a deposit guaranteeing our inheritance..." Ephesians 1:13-14.*

Breath

When we are breathing it shows that we are alive – breath is essential for our natural life: *"The Lord God... breathed into his nostrils the breath of life, and the man became a living being"*

Genesis 2:7. In just the same way, the Holy Spirit is essential for our spiritual life: *"And with that Jesus breathed on them, and said: "Receive the Holy Spirit..." John 20:22.*

Light

We need light in order to see both naturally and spiritually. God himself is described as light: *"In him here is no darkness at all" 1 John 1:5.* We were *"...called out of darkness into his wonderful light" 1 Peter 2:9,* and as the psalmist also reminds us *"The Lord is my light..." Ps 27:1.* We know that this light comes to us through the presence in us of the Holy Spirit of God, which is why Jesus encourages us to: *"let your light shine before men, that they may see your good deeds and praise your Father in heaven" Matthew 5:16.* The Holy Spirit shines God's light into our hearts and minds.

Each of these different symbols tells us something important about the Holy Spirit, and offers us clues to the ways he will work in our lives.

The Person of the Holy Spirit

It is, however, vital from the standpoint of our attitude to him to know that the Holy Spirit is a Divine Person just as much as Jesus and the Father, and therefore worthy to receive our love, adoration and worship; someone in whom we can trust and put our faith. We must not see the Spirit as just a remote channel of power that we in our weakness must plug into and use, but as a person with infinite wisdom, holiness and tenderness, who we need to invite to be actively involved in our lives, working in us and through us. The Greek word Paraclete, often used to describe the Spirit, means one who is by our side to help us. We need to develop a relationship with the Holy Spirit. Those who have come to know him as a person will testify to the blessing he brought into their lives when he came, not just as a warm feeling, but as an ever-present, loving friend and helper, a counsellor and advocate, as promised by Jesus: *"I will ask the Father, and he will give you another Counsellor to be with you forever – the Spirit of truth" John 14:16.*

As St Paul explains in 1 Corinthians 3:16 *"Don't you know that you are God's temple and that God's Spirit lives in you?"*

In the Catholic Catechism section 221, the Church expresses this relationship in these words: **"By sending his only Son and the Spirit of Love in the fullness of time, God has revealed his innermost secret: God himself is an eternal exchange of love, Father, Son, and Holy Spirit, and he has destined us to share in that exchange."**

Every time we recite the Creed, we remind ourselves that the Holy Spirit **"proceeds from the Father and the Son, and that together with them he is worshipped and glorified"**. We know, too, that we do not just receive the Spirit when we are baptised and confirmed, but that he is constantly being poured out, proceeding from God who is always giving him to equip us for life as Christians:

"For God did not call us to be impure, but to live a holy life. Therefore, he who rejects this instruction does not reject man but God, who gives you his Holy Spirit" 1 Thessalonians 4:8.

When we begin to see the Holy Spirit as a person in his own right who wants to be in relationship with us, we will be more open to a change in our approach to him, and the process of transforming our lives can begin.

IS THERE A CLEAR DISTINCTION IN THE BIBLE BETWEEN THE FATHER, THE SON, AND THE HOLY SPIRIT?

Yes, there are clear distinctions between the three persons, and it is evident that they each have quite distinct personalities. They have a definite relationship with each other, they speak of and to one another, they have particular roles and work to do, whilst at the same time they are in total unity.

- In *Luke 3:21-22,* when Jesus is baptised by John, there is a clear distinction between Jesus who comes out of the water, the Father who speaks affirming words from heaven, and the Spirit who descends upon Jesus in the physical form of a dove.

- In *John 14:16* when Jesus tells his disciples about the coming of the Spirit, there is again a clear distinction between Jesus who will ask, the Father who will answer, and the Spirit of truth who will be given as the answer: *"And I will ask the Father, and he will give you another Counsellor to be with you forever".*

- In *Matthew 28:19,* the last words Jesus speaks to his disciples clearly identify the three distinct persons of God: *"Therefore go and make disciples of all nations, baptising them*

in the name of the Father and of the Son and of the Holy Spirit,
and teaching them to obey everything I have commanded you."

• In *Acts 2:33*, Peter explains to the crowds gathered in
Jerusalem for Pentecost what it is that they have just
experienced: *"Exalted to the right hand of God, he (Jesus) has*
received from the Father the promised Holy Spirit and has
poured out what you now see and hear".

• Finally, in *John 16:5-16*, Jesus tells his followers that he must
go back to the Father, but that the Spirit will come in his place
to be with them: *"Now I am going to him who sent me... unless*
I go away the Counsellor will not come to you... but when
he, the Spirit of truth, comes, he will guide you into all truth".

In the **Catholic Catechism section 689** we are reminded that:
"When the Father sends his Word, he always sends his Breath.
In their joint mission, the Son and the Holy Spirit are distinct but
inseperable. It is Christ who is seen, the visible image of the
invisible God, but it is the Spirit who reveals him. The one
whom the Father has sent into our hearts, the Spirit of his Son, is
truly God. Consubstantial with the Father and the Son, the Spirit
is inseperable from them."

So although the doctrine of the Trinity is not directly and
specifically taught in the Scriptures, it is accepted by putting
together a number of facts which are clearly taught. From these we
know there is one God, but there are three distinct, equal, and
divine persons in this one God - the Father, the Son, and the Holy
Spirit. But Karl Rahner's 1967 book called **'The Trinity'**, published
by Burns and Oates in English in 1970, caused a big reaction among

theologians. In it, Rahner expressed the view that in spite of claiming belief in the Trinity, many Christians give very little thought to the three distinct persons in the Godhead. In Rahner's words **"should the doctrine of the Trinity have to be dropped as false, the major part of religious literature could well remain virtually unchanged"**.

Perhaps we need to ask ourselves if in practice the doctrine of the Trinity really makes any difference to the lives of most Christians, as this may help to explain why so many people hardly ever think about the personality of the Holy Spirit, or the clearly defined work he wants to do in their lives.

IS THE HOLY SPIRIT LESS IMPORTANT THAN THE FATHER AND JESUS?

Whilst the answer to this question is definitely no, it's easy to understand why someone asks it. When we look at the number of theological books written on the Trinity, we quickly see that a relatively small proportion is devoted to the Holy Spirit. When I ask people which are the most important Christian feast days, I always hear about Christmas and Easter, but only occasionally about Pentecost. In my school days, apart from during the weeks preceding my Confirmation, I can hardly remember any systematic teaching on the Holy Spirit. All these things may therefore cause us to ask if the Spirit is less important, less than equal, and in some strange way less divine, than God the Father and God the Son? Of course this is nonsense, the three persons of God are equal in every way, but how are we to present a clear picture of the Holy Spirit to make clear his equality and importance?

The Scriptures tell us that the Spirit has four divine attributes:

He is eternal   *"...through the eternal Spirit... Hebrews 9:14*
He is omnipresent *"Where can I go from your Spirit?"*
                      Psalm 139: 7-10
He is omnipotent *"You will receive power when the Holy*
                      Spirit comes on you... Acts 1:8
He is omniscient *"...he will guide you into all truth"*
                      John 16:13

And that he carries out three divine works:

Creates   *"... the Spirit of God was hovering over*
                     the waters" Gen 1:2
Gives life   *"The Spirit gives life..." John 6:63*
Inspires prophecy *"...men spoke from God as they were carried*
                      along by the Holy Spirit" 2 Peter
1:21

Scripture also shows us that his name is coupled with those of the Father and the Son in a way that expresses full equality and divinity:

"May the grace of the Lord Jesus Christ, and the love of God, and the fellowship of the Holy Spirit be with you all" 2 Corinthians 13:14.

And that lying to the Holy Spirit is lying to God:

In *Acts 5:3-4*, when Peter addresses Ananias, he speaks of lying to the Holy Spirit and lying to God as one and the same *"you have*

lied to the Holy Spirit ...you have not lied to men but to God".
From these simple examples of the divine attributes, the divine works, the linking of the Spirit with the Father and the Son, and the fact that he is called God, we can see that the Holy Spirit is a person, distinct from the Father and Son, but fully and equally divine. He cannot, therefore, be any less important, and so it is entirely appropriate to worship and adore him, to pray to and through him, and to enter into a living and dynamic relationship with him. For those who may wish to look into all this in greater depth, I suggest:

- a study of the Holy Spirit in the new Catechism of the Catholic Church.
- a look at the writings of Pope John Paul II on the Holy Spirit
- a Bible study of the numerous references to the Spirit in the Old and New Testaments, including **Joel 2: 28-29, John chapters 14, 15, 16.**

St. Augustine also offers us three helpful insights into the Holy Spirit:
- **he is the unifying love and communion in the Trinity**
- **he is the love that persists and lasts**
- **he is both the Giver and the Gift.**

WHAT IS THE HOLY SPIRIT'S PERSONALITY - WHAT DOES HE DO?

Should we be thinking of the Holy Spirit in the same way we think of Jesus, and therefore behaving towards him as a loving, wise, and tender person? Yes, I'm sure we should. In *John 14:16-17* Jesus tells his disciples that he will not leave them orphans, and that the Spirit will come to them in his place. They must have wondered how anyone, not least an unknown Holy Spirit, could possibly be anything like Jesus. They were to find out on the Day of Pentecost.

So how personal and how present to us is the Holy Spirit?

He has personal characteristics:

Knowledge	*"...no-one knows the thoughts of God except the Spirit of God" 1 Cor.2:11*
Will	*"...and he gives them to each one just as he determines" 1 Cor. 12:11*
Love	*"...and by the love of the Spirit..." Romans 15:30*
Grief	*"I urge you brothers, do not grieve the Holy Spirit of God" Eph. 4:30*

He acts as a person:

Searches	*"The Spirit searches all things even the deep things of God" 1 Cor.2:10*
Speaks	*"...the Holy Spirit spoke through the mouth of David..." Acts 1:16*
Calls out	*"...the Spirit who calls out "Abba, Father" Galatians 4:6*
Intercedes	*"...the Spirit himself intercedes for us..." Romans 8:26*
Teaches	*"...the Holy Spirit... will teach you all things..." John 14:26*
Leads	*"...because those who are led by the Spirit of God..." Romans 8:14*

Commands	*"The Spirit told Philip..." Acts 8:29*
Appoints	*"...all the flock of which the Spirit has made you overseers" Acts 20:28*
Forbids	*"The Spirit of Jesus would not allow them to..." Acts 16:6-7*

He is treated as a person:

Rebelled against	*"Yet they rebelled and grieved his Holy Spirit" Isaiah 63:10*
Insulted	*"...who has insulted the Spirit of grace?" Hebrews 10:29*
Lied to	*"...that you have lied to the Holy Spirit..." Acts 5:3*
Blasphemed against	*"...blasphemy against the Spirit will not be forgiven"Mt.12:31*
Resisted	*"You always resist the Holy Spirit!" Acts 7:51*

We can also notice that in every translation of the Bible, the personal pronoun 'he' is used when referring to the Holy Spirit – a practice I am following in this book.

He has particular work to do:

Creating	*"The Spirit of God has made me" Job 33:4*
Witnessing	*"We are witnesses... so is the Holy Spirit" Acts 5:32*
Convicting of sin	*"He will convict the world... in regard to sin" John 16:8-11*
Making us new	*"saved through... And renewal by the Holy Spirit" Titus 3:4-5*
Setting us free	*"The law of the Spirit of life set me free"*

	Romans 8:2
Strengthening us	*"...strengthen you with power through his Spirit" Eph. 3:16*
Leading us	*"...those who are led by the Spirit of God" Romans 8:14*
Producing fruit	*"The fruit of the Spirit is love, joy, peace..." Galatians 5:22*
Supporting us	*"...the Spirit is given for the common good" 1 Cor.12:7*
Distributing gifts	*"To one there is given through the Spirit..." 1 Cor. 12:1-11*
Protecting us	*"kept by the Spirit from preaching in Asia" Acts 16:6*
Reminding us	*"will remind you of everything I have said to you" John 14:26*

These are just some examples, and we can find many other ways that the Holy Spirit is at work. But above all, his purpose is to reveal Jesus to us, and in order to ensure that Jesus is lifted up, he makes himself less conspicuous. Perhaps this is one of the reasons we lose sight of his work, his power, his authority and his importance.

Jesus is Lord, God is our loving Father

So far in this chapter we have seen that the Holy Spirit is a person, distinct from but co-equal with the Father and Son. He has a particular and necessary work to do in each one of us, but will wait until we invite him to come to us and take control of our lives. When he comes, he will reveal Jesus as a living Lord in a wonderful new way. So often the excitement of the present-day, miracle-working Lord is missing because our eyes are fixed on what happened during the earthly ministry of Jesus. So we have no real concept of a living, contemporary Lord present in our lives, and wanting to work through us to reach out and touch those around us. Through the ministry of the Holy Spirit, many are discovering this glorious experience anew, and it is the Spirit's desire to come to us as a loving friend and helper, so that he can point us to the living Jesus as Lord, and to God as our loving Father. In *1 Corinthians 12:3* Paul reminds us *"No one can say 'Jesus is Lord' except by the Holy Spirit", and in Romans 8:16 "The Spirit himself testifies with our spirit that we are God's children".*

If we allow Him, the Spirit will securely anchor us in these two key relationships. He is the Spirit of unity, and we really need to know him well and to allow him to work in us and through us. But unless we believe in him, knowing that when we ask he will be given, we will never ask and so will not experience his life-changing presence.

ARE WE NOW GIVING TOO MUCH EMPHASIS TO THE HOLY SPIRIT?

This is a cause of concern for some people, and perhaps in order to correct a deficiency, a need has been felt to over-compensate. But the Spirit himself always points us to Jesus and the Father - he is like a spotlight, and we should certainly not be gazing into the spotlight but at the ones held in the light. If we stare into the spotlight, we become dazzled and unable to see clearly, but we need the spotlight to focus our attention on the full wonder and glory of the person of Jesus, and to help us see God as our loving

Father. Without the Holy Spirit freely at work in us, our understanding of Jesus and the Father will remain limited, and we will find ourselves trying to live the Christian life without the power God provides to make it possible. Because the Holy Spirit does not draw attention to himself, someone has to do it for him, otherwise he may well be overlooked. One of God's purposes in the 20th century outpourings of the Holy Spirit called **Pentecostalism** and the **Charismatic Renewal**, is to demonstrate, through millions of men and women all over the world, the life-changing effects of a new experience of the love and activity of the Holy Spirit, revealed to us through these grass-roots explosions of supernatural power.

Heavenly power has come to earth

To look at this in another way, there are Christians who know they have Jesus beside them, and there are others who know they must be in Jesus, with his life inside them through the presence of the Holy Spirit. The first group tries to handle the problems of life in their own strength with an occasional prayer for divine help, whereas group two knows that on their own they are helpless, but with the person and presence of God living in them through the Holy Spirit, heavenly power has come to earth and will be effective if they surrender to it. They have understood they must be in Jesus:

"Remain in me, and I will remain in you. No branch can bear fruit by itself; it must remain in the vine. Neither can you bear fruit unless you remain in me. I am the vine; you are the branches. If a man remains in me and I in him, he will bear much fruit; apart from me, you can do nothing" John 15 verses 4 and 5.

This second group knows that their life is now in Christ, and that the Holy Spirit living in them is the sign and guarantee of this. The inside life, us in Jesus and Jesus in us, is what the Holy Spirit will bring about in each of us – if we allow him to. He will not force himself upon us, but our clear YES will mean that his power is released within us and we are filled with the utter fullness of God. Because some people have not understood this, we need to clearly teach the vital role of the Holy Spirit in the life of every Christian, and to bring about a proper balance in our appreciation of the importance and work of all three persons of the Trinity - Father, Son, and Spirit.

Above all, the working of the Spirit in us must be visible to others – we have to embody the message and the experience, to be living examples. Why is this important? Because people **"will listen more willingly to witnesses than to teachers, and if they listen to teachers it is because they are witnesses"**, words of **Pope John Paul II** in his document **Ecclesia in Europa, 49.**

Ask for the Good Gift

But even if we have been baptised and confirmed, we may still be unaware of the need to personally and deliberately invite the Holy Spirit to be at work in our lives - we have to ask, as *Luke* tells us in *chapter 11 verses 9-13:*

"So I say to you: Ask and it will be given to you; seek and you will find; knock and the door will be opened to you. For everyone who asks receives; he who seeks finds; and to him who knocks, the door will be opened. Which of you fathers, if your son asks for a fish, will give him a snake instead? Or if he asks for an egg, will give him a scorpion? If you then, though you are evil, know how to give good gifts to your children, how much more will your Father in

heaven give the Holy Spirit to those who ask him!"
How all this relates to our Baptism and Confirmation will be addressed in the coming chapters, but in the above Scripture Jesus is making it very clear - the Holy Spirit is the good gift our Father longs to give us, but the gift is given *"...to those who ask him"*. Why do we need the gift? Because there is work to be done that only the Holy Spirit can do. Sadly, so many are unaware of this that there is a real need today to talk about the person and work of the Spirit in order that people will find a new desire to live a fuller life in the Holy Spirit, and more and more will decide to ask, discovering to their great surprise that when they do, the Holy Spirit is given in an amazing new way. But if we are like the disciples Paul encountered at Ephesus in *Acts 19:2 "we have not even heard that there is a Holy Spirit"*, or if we have never understood that the gift of the Holy Spirit has been given, we won't even know we can ask for it. The reason we need to give more emphasis to the Holy Spirit is to correct the weaknesses and ignorance that have crept into the understanding of so many in the Church today, thereby undermining his work in our lives.

When God makes promises, he keeps them – think of Abram, Mary, or Peter. He has given us himself in the person of Jesus, and where Jesus is, his Spirit is also - the two are "conjoined and inseparable" as the **Catholic Catechism 689** and **743** expresses it. In the words of Jesus in the *Book of Revelation 22:17: "Come! Whoever is thirsty, let him come; and whoever wishes let him take the free gift of the water of life"*.

This water of life is the Holy Spirit, a gift freely offered to all who will accept him.

Come, Holy Spirit!

Discuss the following statements with reference to the Scriptures:

**The Holy Spirit is a person
to whom we can relate**

**He is God, and therefore to be
loved, worshipped, and adored**

**He is quite distinct from the
Father and the Son, but co-equal**

**He has a vital job to do in the life of
every member of the body of Christ**

The Scriptures:

John 14:15-31 and Luke 3: 21-22

The Questions:

**What is the vital work the Holy Spirit
needs to do in me now?**

**Have I ever deliberately invited
him to work freely in my life?**

CHAPTER TWO

THE PROMISE OF
THE HOLY SPIRIT

- **Where do we find the Promise and who makes the Promise?**
- **What is promised and to whom is the Promise made?**
- **When can we receive the Promise?**
- **What questions might we ask ourselves to find out if we need the help of the Holy Spirit?**

So far we have seen that the Holy Spirit is a person in his own right, distinct from the Father and the Son; that he is God, co-equal, and therefore worthy to receive our love and adoration. When we invite him he comes as an ever-present friend and helper, and his particular ministry is to reveal Jesus as our living Lord and Saviour, God as our loving Father, and to equip us to live a full Christian life.

WHERE DO WE FIND THE PROMISE AND WHO MAKES THE PROMISE?

We first find the Promise in the Old Testament

The Old Testament prophets were specially chosen for their ministries, and they and certain priests and kings received the Spirit in part – not the fullness, only a 'measure' of the Spirit -- to equip them for what God called them to do. Almost all the prophets pointed to the widespread outpouring of the Holy Spirit that would one day come. They spoke of God giving his people a new heart and a new spirit, but it was only at Pentecost that the Holy Spirit became available to all people in his fullness, just as they had prophesied. Here are a few examples of their prophecies:

All God's people will one day be empowered by the Spirit:
"I will pour out my Spirit on your offspring...." Isaiah 44:3
"And afterward, I will pour out my Spirit on all people" Joel 2:28
"I will give you a new heart and put a new spirit in you" Ezekiel 36:26

The Messiah will be empowered by the Spirit:
"Here is my servant... my chosen one... I will put my Spirit on him..." Isaiah 42:1

The New Covenant will be in the Spirit:
"I will put my Spirit in you... you will be my people... Ezekiel 36:26-29

We find the Promise repeated and amplified in the New Testament, where it is first fulfilled in Jesus

He is conceived by the power of the Holy Spirit:
"The Holy Spirit will come upon you..." Luke 1:35

He is anointed with the Holy Spirit after his Baptism by John:
"...and the Holy Spirit descended on him in bodily form like a dove" Luke 3:22

He is led by the Spirit into the desert:
"Jesus, full of the Holy Spirit, returned from the Jordan and was led by the Spirit in the desert..." Luke 4:1

He comes out of the desert *"in the power of the Spirit" Luke 4:14*

He demonstrates the power of the Spirit in his public ministry:
"...I drive out demons by the Spirit of God..." Matthew 12:28

John the Baptist, who received the Spirit at his birth *Luke 1:15*, and is described by Jesus as *"more than a prophet" Luke 7:26*, tells us that in Jesus there is not only forgiveness and cleansing from sin, but also that through him the fire of the Holy Spirit will be released: *"He will baptise you with the Holy Spirit and with fire" Luke 3:16.*

Jesus promises his disciples that they will receive the Holy Spirit:
"I will ask the Father, and he will give you... the Spirit of truth" John 14:16
"...when he, the Spirit of truth comes..." John 16:13
"...the Spirit will take from what is mine and make it known to you" John 16:15

SO WHO MAKES THE PROMISE?

God our Father makes the Promise

The Holy Spirit is the promised gift of the Father, released to us by the work of Jesus. Before we could receive the Spirit, Jesus had to die, rise from the dead, and return to his Father. When Jesus spoke about leaving them in *John chapter 16* his disciples were afraid - their lives revolved around him and his physical presence among them, so they were unable to see what could possibly be better than this, and we would almost certainly have felt the same. They had no idea they were about to enter a new period of history, *The Age of the Holy Spirit,* the age in which we are now living, when God himself is present in the heart and life of every Christian through the person of the Holy Spirit, given to us on the Day of Pentecost.

After Jesus had ascended the disciples waited in Jerusalem for the Father's gift:
"...the gift my Father promised" Acts 1:4.
"I am going to send you what my Father has promised" Luke 24:49
"When the Counsellor comes... from the Father" John 15:26
"...he (Jesus) has received from the Father the promised Holy Spirit..." Acts 2:33
"...how much more will your Father in heaven give the Holy Spirit..." Luke 11:13

Jesus promised that the Spirit, the helper, would be with us always:
"I will ask the Father, and he will give you another Counsellor to be with you forever – the Spirit of truth" John 14:16.

So there is no need to be lonely or afraid, hopeless or helpless ever again. We are never orphans *John 14:18,* the Father and the Son are here in us through the presence of the Holy Spirit. He is with us every moment of our lives and he is enough – we need nothing more. To put it another way – the glorified Jesus is not just with us but also in us, working from the inside outwards to transform our lives. This is what happened on Pentecost Day, when the Promise of the Spirit was fulfilled.

WHAT IS PROMISED AND TO WHOM IS THE PROMISE MADE?

"The Spirit of truth – to be with you forever" John 14:16.

Not:
- just a set of gifts
- a particular experience
- a warm feeling
- a religious ritual

But:
- the person
- the presence
- the love
- the power
- the new life of God himself, released in us here and now in the Spirit

Why?
- to renew us inwardly and outwardly
- to renew us in our relationships with God, ourselves, and others
- to renew us in our Christian witness
- to make us holy (after all, he is the Holy Spirit)

So the Promise is the gift to us of the Holy Spirit, God himself, to renew and change us, to equip us to live the Christian life.

The Promise is made to those who ask:

"....how much more will your Father in heaven give the Holy Spirit to those who ask him!" Luke 11:13 and *"If anyone is thirsty, let him come to me and drink"* John 7:37-39

If we receive the Holy Spirit as part of our Christian initiation, why are we exhorted to ask, to come and to drink? Because we must make a positive and personal response to the gift we've been given – we must say a definitive YES to what we've received. Only then is the love and power of the Spirit within us fully released and effective, and this may not have happened when we were baptised and confirmed.

The Promise is to all who repent and are baptised:

Peter challenges the crowd on Pentecost Day, 3,000 people respond, are baptised and receive the Holy Spirit: *"Repent and be baptised, every one of you, in the name of Jesus for the forgiveness of your sins. And you will receive the gift of the Holy Spirit"* Acts 2:38. Repentance and Baptism will normally precede the giving of the Holy Spirit.

"The promise is for you and your children and for all who are far off – for all whom the Lord our God will call" Acts 2:39.

So the Promise is made to us when we ask, when we repent, when we are baptised, and when we respond to the Lord's call.

It is made:
   - **to us and our children**
   - **to all who are far off**
   - **to those the Lord calls**

WHEN CAN WE RECEIVE THE PROMISE?

When we become Christians and are baptised:
"Repent and be baptised... and you will receive the gift of the Holy Spirit" Acts 2:38

When we ask:
"after they prayed... they were all filled with the Holy Spirit and spoke the word of God boldly" Acts 4:31

When the Father fulfils the Promise:
The Father poured out the *'power from on high'*, and the disciples and Mary were *'baptised in the Holy Spirit' Acts 1: 4-5; Acts 1: 8; Acts 2:1-4; Luke 24:49.*

The same Promise is later fulfilled for the Gentiles:
"While Peter was still speaking these words, the Holy Spirit came on all who heard the message. The circumcised believers (Jews) who had come with Peter were astonished that the gift of the Holy Spirit had been poured out even on the Gentiles" Acts 10: 44-45.

When the Church prays:
Peter and John were sent down to Samaria, and *"when they arrived they prayed for them that they might receive the Holy Spirit" Acts 8:14-17.*

When God heals:
In *Acts 9:15-19* we read how Ananias is sent to the blind Saul, *"so that you may see again and be filled with the Holy Spirit"*

and " He got up and was baptised..."

Paul assumes that all Christians have received and are availing themselves of the Spirit and his power:

"You, however, are controlled, not by the sinful nature but by the Spirit, if the Spirit of God lives in you. And if anyone does not have the Spirit of Christ, he does not belong to Christ" Romans 8:9-10.

But for many of us there is still a question to answer - not about receiving but about availing. Have we thrown open the doors and windows of our lives to the fresh, empowering wind of the Holy Spirit?

The gift to us of the Holy Spirit is the fulfilment of the promise, but with the Holy Spirit there is a **now** and a **not yet**. The Spirit has started in us, and the fact that he has started is the guarantee of completion. *"Having believed, you were marked in him (Christ) with a seal, the promised Holy Spirit, who is a deposit guaranteeing our inheritance..." Ephesians 1:13-14.* But if we think of the above text *Romans 8:9-10* the extent to which we are *"controlled by the Spirit"* will depend on the extent to which we have surrendered our lives to his control. Many of us in whom the **Spirit of God lives** may not be **controlled** by the Spirit because there are areas of our lives we have not yet surrendered. We must give the power back to God in every part of our lives and leave it with him. To do this we need to be constantly re-filled with the Holy Spirit so that we are transformed into the Lord's likeness, *2 Corinthians 3:18.*

We receive the Promise when we ask:

"Whoever is thirsty, let him come; and whoever wishes, let him take the free gift of the water of life" Revelation 22:17. God is the one who gives us everything in creation, but he goes even further and gives us himself. The gift is Jesus and the Spirit of Jesus, as we saw earlier the two are conjoined and inseparable **(Catechism 689).** Paul urges all of us to renew our experience of the Holy Spirit, to be filled again and again: *"...be filled with the Spirit..." Ephesians 5:18.* The use here in the original text of the aorist tense of the verb 'filled' implies that we need to go on being filled, and this was certainly the experience of the early Christian Community *Acts 4:31.*

Keep being filled...

In *Acts 4:31* we see that as the disciples prayed for boldness in proclaiming the word of God *"...they were all filled with the Holy Spirit and spoke the word of God boldly".* This is only a short time after they were all filled on the Day of Pentecost.

It's really important to note that these early disciples continued to pray regularly to be filled again with the Spirit – so should we. The full release of the Spirit in our lives is not something that happens automatically through our Christian initiation. Yes, we receive the Holy Spirit, but unless our response is wholehearted, the out-working of the grace is restricted, and when our expectation is low, little will happen.

We cannot assume today that because someone has been baptised and confirmed they are fully alive in the Spirit – this is more likely to be the exception rather than the rule. It's why we regularly need to pray for and receive a new outpouring of the Spirit. This should not be seen as a second blessing but as a recovery of an unrealised part of the original blessing – the grace we received at Baptism. More on this later, in the chapter on Baptism in the Holy Spirit.

Jamie Buckingham, a very practical American spiritual writer, explains how we should understand being filled with the Spirit in his book entitled **'Power for Living'**, sponsored and published in 1985 by the Arthur S. De Moss Foundation. Jamie explains our need to be filled like this:

"At the very moment you were born again the Holy Spirit took up residence in your life. However, that does not mean you are filled with the Holy Spirit. To be filled means that you are controlled and empowered. It means you are relying on the power of God to change your life, rather than trying to do it yourself. Power for living is yours only when you yield to him and let him control your life. You cannot live the Christian life in your own power through self-determination and self-discipline. Only Jesus was able to live a perfect life, and only as he lives in you through his Spirit can you live victoriously. In a nutshell, to be filled with the Holy Spirit means to be filled with Jesus".

Has the Spirit got me?

Cardinal Leon Josef Suenens, one of the key figures of the Second Vatican Council, explained it in a similarly simple way. He said that the question we need to ask ourselves is not "have I got the Spirit?" because if we've been baptised we have got the Spirit. The question we must ask is "has the Spirit got me?" Do I know for certain that I have clearly and unequivocally given him permission to be in control and to direct my life? Did I even realise that I'm supposed to do that? If not, I need to do it without delay.

Many of us had to wait to experience the fullness of the Holy Spirit until we had been Christians for many years. So could we not have received all that was available at the time of our conversion to Christ or our initiation into the Church? YES, we could and we did - but we didn't understand the fullness of what we received because no one had taught us or told us, so we didn't expect much to happen. Or perhaps we were told but lacked the faith to fully receive what God was giving - if only we had believed in the *streams of living water* Jesus speaks of in *John 7: 37-39* we could have moved from living on spiritual snacks to enjoying lavish banquets years ago! The Holy Spirit really is the Church's best-kept secret. If we ask what the Church needs most, the answer must be **"the power of the Holy Spirit."**

Pope Paul VI's answer was unequivocal: **"...the Spirit, the Holy Spirit... the Church needs her perennial Pentecost; she needs fire in her heart, words on her lips, prophecy in her outlook"**. Some will remember the prayer **Pope John XXIII** asked the whole Church to pray before the Second Vatican Council: **"Lord, renew your wonders in this our day as by a new Pentecost!"**

How will the Church experience a new Pentecost?

When most baptised people are fully alive in the grace of the sacrament, empowered for discipleship, and open to the Holy Spirit day by day.

Here are some questions we might ask ourselves to see if we need more help from the Holy Spirit:

- What evidence is there of the Spirit's work in my life? *Romans 8:5*
- Am I ever aware of the inner prompting of the Holy Spirit? *Acts 16:6-8*
- Is Jesus real to me as a person and as my Lord? *1 Peter 3:15*
- Am I secure in my relationship as a child of the Father? *Romans 8:15-16*
- Do I see in myself a love for other people, and do I have a concern and care for people I would not normally choose as friends? *1 John 4:11-12*
- Do I find there are times when words I am saying really touch and help someone with a problem? *1 Corinthians 12:8*
- Am I ready to talk to others about my Christian faith? *Matthew 10:8.*
- Do I receive help when I pray? *Romans 8:26-27*
- Is there a new excitement when I read the Bible? *Hebrews 4:12-13*
- Is there a new freedom in praising & worshipping God? *Ephesians 1:3-14*
- Is the Eucharist at the centre of my spiritual life? *1 Corinthians 11:23-26, and Catholic Catechism, 1324*
- Am I growing in holiness, *"the essential pre-requisite for evangelisation?"* Ecclesia in Europa 49, John Paul II's document on the Church in Europe.
- Do I feel a need to put on the full armour of God? *Ephesians 6:12-18.*

- **Am I exercising any of the spiritual gifts?**
  1 Corinthians 12:7
- **Is the fruit of the Spirit evident in my life?**
  Galatians 5:22-23
- **Am I playing an active part in the life of my local church?** *Acts 2:46-47*
- **Have I ever really asked God for his gift, for the fullness of the Holy Spirit?** *Luke 11:9-13.*

These questions are designed to reveal to us how much evidence there is of the Spirit's presence and work in our lives, and reference to the Scriptures will help our understanding of how we might recognise this.

The Holy Spirit was promised in the Old Testament, revealed in the life of Jesus, and poured out on the infant church on Pentecost Day. He is the gift of God our Father, and is available in his fullness to all who ask, and that obviously includes us!

Come, Holy Spirit!

Discuss the following statements with reference to the Scriptures:

The Holy Spirit is the gift of the Father, promised to his children, and released after the Ascension of Jesus

The Promise is the gift of God himself, here and now, given to renew, empower and change us

The Promise is made to every member of God's family

We need the fullness of the Holy Spirit if we are to live effective Christian lives in the love and power of God

The Scriptures:

Joel: 2: 28-29 and John 16: 5-16

The Questions:

Have I received the fullness of the Holy Spirit, and if so, what evidence is there in my life?

Write down your answers to each of the questions on pages 42 and 43

CHAPTER THREE

BAPTISED IN THE HOLY SPIRIT

- **Why do we talk about being Baptised in the Holy Spirit, and how does it relate to our Baptism and Confirmation?**
- **How do we describe Baptism in the Holy Spirit?**
- **How can we receive this new life in the Spirit?**
- **Are there any hindrances to receiving it?**
- **What is likely to happen after we have received this gift from God?**

We have seen that the Holy Spirit is a person in his own right, the gift of the Father released to us by Jesus, and he comes to us at the time of our Christian initiation. Subsequent to this, he also comes whenever we ask him as a friend and helper, equipping and empowering us to live the Christian life, revealing Jesus as a living Lord and Saviour, and God as our loving Father. He is the source of the new life that will transform us, and all we have to do is ask him to come. When this happens, we may say that we have been baptised in the Spirit, using the phrase we find in several places in the New Testament. People often speak of 'the Baptism in the Spirit' – a phrase not found in the Scriptures, but one which is generally accepted and in common usage, as it is of course directly derived from the verb *baptised in the Spirit*. But in my opinion it is probably better to avoid using 'the', as this suggests a unique event, whereas the Lord may pour out his Spirit upon us time and again. As being filled with the Spirit should be an on-going experience, it fits well to use the verb form *baptised in the Spirit*, which is active and dynamic. But in nearly all the English-speaking world the most used phrase is *Baptism in the Spirit*, whereas in France, Italy, and Spain the normal descriptions are *Effusion de l'Esprit, Effusione dello Spirito, Efusion del Espiritu*, all of which we would probably translate as *Outpouring of the Spirit*. In this chapter we will consider the relationship between baptism in water and Baptism in the Spirit, explained in these words by **St. Augustine: "The Spirit is promised not only to him who does not have, but also to him who already has. For it is given to one who has not, in order that he may have; and to the one who has, that he may have more abundantly," Tractates on the Gospel of John, 74.2.**

WHY DO WE TALK ABOUT BEING 'BAPTISED IN THE HOLY SPIRIT'? WHAT DOES IT REALLY MEAN, AND HOW DOES IT RELATE TO OUR SACRAMENTAL BAPTISM AND CONFIRMATION?

We talk about being **Baptised in the Holy Spirit** because the phrase is used in the New Testament by John the Baptist *Luke 3:16* and by Jesus *Acts 1:5*:

"John answered them all, I baptise you with water. But one more

powerful than I will come… He will baptise you with the Holy Spirit and with fire" Luke 3:16.
Jesus told his disciples:
"For John baptised with water, but in a few days you will be baptised with the Holy Spirit" Acts 1:5.

We see what Jesus means by this most clearly in the account in *Acts 2:1-4* of the coming of the Holy Spirit to the disciples of Jesus, and Mary his mother, on the Day of Pentecost. They were all filled with the Spirit and completely transformed:

"Suddenly a sound like the blowing of a violent wind came from heaven and filled the whole house where they were sitting. They saw what seemed to be tongues of fire that separated and came to rest on each of them. All of them were filled with the Holy Spirit and began to speak in other tongues as the Spirit enabled them".

We look to Pentecost as the birthday of the Church – they were no longer just a group of individual followers of Jesus, they were now a community with a mission. The immediate result is clearly evident in Peter, who fearlessly and confidently preaches an amazing sermon, resulting in 3,000 converts to Christianity. The rough, tough, ignorant fisherman has been transformed into a preacher whose every word is filled with conviction and passion. Today we may debate how to describe what happens when we receive the Holy Spirit, when and how it should occur, and what we should call it – but we can never doubt that something life-changing is supposed to happen, which in many ways will resemble the experience of the first disciples at Pentecost.

Baptised in the Holy Spirit

When we are baptised, whether as babies or as adults, we receive the Holy Spirit, and our Christian initiation is completed with a special coming of the Spirit at our Confirmation. There is no disagreement about this, and on neither occasion do we normally hear people speak about being *baptised in the Holy Spirit*. But when someone subsequently makes a special act of surrendering himself or herself to the Holy Spirit inviting him to take control of their lives, and a change in the person is very quickly evident, we do speak of that person being *baptised in the Holy Spirit*. This is what we are trying to address - what happens and how do we explain it?

Two ways of explaining Baptism in the Holy Spirit:

There are two schools of thought about Baptism in the Holy Spirit, and I think there are good arguments for both. I'm not a theologian, and I don't see that the two views are exclusive, but rather complementary.

God is sovereign, and he often acts outside the boundaries we try to lay down. Many people have experienced dramatic changes in their lives after they have been prayed with for Baptism in the Holy Spirit. They attribute these changes to that specific prayer because they recognise that there is a new power at work in them and through them, helping them to live out their Christian lives with greater commitment and effectiveness. The experience happens – the theological explanations follow.

The first school of thought

Baptism in the Holy Spirit is a release of the graces received through the sacraments of Christian initiation - Baptism and Confirmation. But why does the grace need to be released? It's an accepted view that the grace of the sacraments received is always present, but sometimes it is restricted. In other words, present in us but constrained, not able to work freely, and not therefore as effective as it could and should be. Why? Because we, the recipients, have not responded as we should. Most of us were baptised as infants before we were capable of believing anything, and it is quite possible that since then we have never personally and fully accepted the Christian commitment made on our behalf by our parents and godparents. When we later received the Sacrament of Confirmation it is again quite likely that this too lacked any deep personal commitment to the Lord on our part, and to living a full Christian life in the power of the Spirit. So we never realised that we were first called to be disciples of Jesus, and then sent out in the power of the Spirit to *"make disciples of all the nations" Matthew 28:19.*

In fact there is little point in going out in response to the Church's call for a new evangelisation if we have not first come to Jesus to receive his new life, and then been empowered and equipped by his Holy Spirit. Those who have been 'sacramentalised' but not evangelised are simply not equipped to play their part in an evangelising Church. Our empowering for mission comes when we embrace the sacrament of our Christian initiation, and open ourselves to the outpouring of the charismatic gifts, freely given as the Spirit decides **(1** *Corinthians 12:11,* **Lumen Gentium 12)** and to be used for the benefit of others. There is an important link between a new Pentecost and a new Evangelisation - the former makes possible the latter.

Baptism in the Holy Spirit can therefore be seen as the moment we say a clear and unequivocal YES to the Holy Spirit we have already received – in other words we might describe it as completing our Christian initiation. Our YES releases the power of the Spirit that was always present within us. Finally we play our part, and in faith affirm the Christian commitment of our Baptism and Confirmation. Baptism in the Spirit, therefore, fans into a flame the gift of God already received *2 Timothy 1:6*.

The relationship between Baptism in the Holy Spirit and the sacraments of Christian initiation is very important. A sacrament is always valid **'ex opere operato'** – in other words, by the very fact that it is given. But the Church also teaches us that the real fruitfulness of the sacrament in someone's life is **'ex opere operantis'**. That means it depends on the following subjective factors:

- the quality of the preparation
- the belief and commitment of the person ministering the sacrament
- the faith, expectation and understanding of the person receiving the sacrament.

If there is little faith and low expectation, not much change or fruit will be evident in the recipient's life. Both Scripture and the writings of the Church Fathers clearly show that the normal results of Baptism and Confirmation were a powerful release of God's love and power, resulting in transformed lives. What then followed was powerful and effective evangelisation, accompanied by the use of charismatic gifts. All this is in direct contrast to what we normally find today, and if we want to see a full release of the power of these sacraments, we need to teach and minister Baptism in the Holy

Spirit. Baptism in the Spirit is never a substitute for the sacraments, but when people ask for a new outpouring of the Spirit and their lives are transformed, they will often refer to Baptism in the Spirit as their moment of real conversion, when they personally met Jesus as their living Lord and Saviour – their personal Pentecost moment.

So although the Spirit was always present, he was hardly noticeable or effective because we were ignorant of the need to surrender to him, or in some cases we simply decided not to do so. When we do surrender, the Spirit within us is suddenly set free, and the full power in the sacraments of our initiation is released – we begin to live committed and courageous Christian lives.

Most of us do not consciously resist the Holy Spirit, as Stephen accused the Sanhedrin of doing *"You always resist the Holy Spirit!" Acts 7:51.* But perhaps we need to hear Paul's exhortation in *1 Thessalonians 5:19 "Do not put out the Spirit's fire"* which is effectively what we are doing when we ignore his presence within us. In this first school of thought, because there has been a total giving of the Spirit when we received the sacraments of Christian initiation, subsequent prayer for Baptism in the Spirit simply results in a conscious experience of the release of that power which has already been received. But this cannot be all that happens for a number of reasons, among which are the following:

- it seems to limit the great prayer **'Veni, Creator Spiritus',** which is prayed by the Catholic Church on so many occasions, inviting the Spirit to come in a new way.

- it seems to question the traditional belief that there is always a new coming of the Spirit at important moments, both sacramental and simply prayerful. For example, when a man is ordained a priest there is a new sending of the Spirit with gifts to equip him for his new ministry, in just the same way as the Spirit comes with the other sacraments. On September 12th 2010 **Pope Benedict XVI** spoke to newly consecrated bishops at Castelgandolfo, Italy, and told them: **"In every task you are sustained by the Holy Spirit, who in ordination configured you to Christ, the Eternal High Priest"**.

• are we also saying that when we pray **'Come, Holy Spirit'** we do not really expect a new outpouring of the Spirit because it happened once and for all when we were baptised? Of course not – the Spirit came then and comes again now.

So whilst it is certain that Baptism in the Holy Spirit releases more of the grace received when we were baptised and confirmed, I am certain there is also always a new sending of the Spirit when we pray **'Come, Holy Spirit!'**

The second school of thought

Baptism in the Holy Spirit is a powerful new sending of the Spirit in response to our invitation. The person asking may well have been baptised and confirmed, but sometimes this may not have happened. Jesus pours out his Holy Spirit in amazing new ways in response to our invitation, and while it may be unusual we can point to occasions in the New Testament when the Spirit is poured out before water baptism has taken place, and also cite examples today of people who are filled with the Spirit without being baptised in water.

When looking at some Evangelical and most Pentecostal experience, we see that when a person prays a prayer of repentance and commitment to Christ, they receive the Holy Spirit and may manifest one or more of the gifts of the Spirit, particularly speaking in tongues. For them, water baptism will often come later. So in this second school of thought, when we ask to be baptised in the Holy Spirit, there is simply a powerful new sending of the Spirit.

In the New Testament, the outpouring of the Spirit always resulted in clear evidence of his presence in the recipients. When Peter miraculously goes to the household of Cornelius, Luke explains the events that followed in *Acts 10: 44-48:*

While Peter was still speaking these words, the Holy Spirit came on all who heard the message. The circumcised believers who had come with Peter were astonished that the gift of the Holy Spirit had been poured out even on the Gentiles. For they heard them speaking in tongues and praising God. Then Peter said, "Can anyone keep these people from being baptised with water? They have received the Holy Spirit just as we have." So he ordered that they be baptised in the name of Jesus Christ.

What occurred here is often described as the Pentecost of the Gentiles.

When Paul writes to the 'foolish' Christians in Galatia, his irritation is caused by the fact that he had seen the Spirit freely working in them, but now they have gone back to relying on their own efforts. We must all be on our guard against this temptation:

"After beginning with the Spirit, are you now trying to attain your goal by human effort? Have you suffered so much for nothing – if it really was for nothing? Does God give you his Spirit and work miracles among you because you observe the law, or because you believe what you heard?" Galatians 3:3-5.

Change validates the experience

These and other New Testament Scriptures indicate that any new sending of the Spirit should result in a noticeable change in the recipients, and the change validates the experience. When in 1976 I experienced the Holy Spirit at work in me in new ways, I realised there had certainly been a new sending or outpouring of the Spirit in response to the prayer that was prayed and my openness to receive. The Anglican priest who prayed over me told me that he believed God was going to change my life. The dramatic nature of the changes that followed would have been impossible without a new outpouring of the Holy Spirit. Yes, the graces of my Baptism and Confirmation were fully at work for the first time, but I am certain there was also a new outpouring of the Spirit to equip me for all that lay ahead. This seems to fit well with the views of St. **Thomas Aquinas in Summa Theologica I :**

"There is an invisible sending also with respect to an advance in virtue or an increase in grace... Such an invisible sending is especially to be seen in that kind of increase in grace whereby a person moves forward into some new act or some new state of grace: as, for instance, when a person moves forward into the grace of working miracles, or of prophecy..."

When we consider this text, it is quite clear that St. Thomas is writing about new sendings of the Spirit to equip people with a special grace for some new activities, and the examples he offers are of charismatic rather than sacramental graces. But it is also clear from the writings of St. Thomas that such new sendings are always related to a change in a person's relationship with God, to a significant move forward. This has been the experience of so many saints and holy men and women, who at profound moments of change or conversion have received a spontaneous new sending of the Spirit, which is not linked to their sacramental baptism. At such moments they have also received special charisms – graces freely given to equip them for new areas of service. This was the experience of Francis of Assisi, Ignatius of Loyola, Teresa of Avila and many others.

The key to receiving lies in asking, and in *James 4:2* we are reminded that sometimes we do not receive from God because we do not ask: *"You do not have because you do not ask God"*. In both schools of thought, inviting the Spirit is the key to receiving.

Can we combine these two schools of thought?

I am at home with both of these schools of thought working together. If, as the first view suggests, we have not availed ourselves of the grace received at our sacramental Baptism and Confirmation, we certainly need to consciously do so, thereby releasing the fullness of the restricted grace. But when we pray **'Come, Holy Spirit'**, we must also be expectant that there will be a new sending of the Spirit, a new outpouring of grace – one that will have immediate and visible effects. I can live with some lack of clarity in the relationship between these two things, releasing and sending, or that which has already been given and that which is newly given, as I have often seen God do things I never expected him to do. So when it comes to the things of the Holy Spirit, I am open to God's surprises. My simple view is that when we speak of Baptism in the Holy Spirit, we are speaking of God working in the lives of individual men and women who come alive in their faith in remarkable new ways. So it seems to me that in this awakening of faith there is certainly a release of what is already present within us, the power of the Holy Spirit received at Baptism, but there is also a new outpouring of the Spirit. After all, the first disciples experienced a remarkable outpouring of the Spirit in the Upper Room on Pentecost Day, but only a short time later they received another filling with the Spirit when they prayed for boldness to preach the word. *"After they prayed, the place where they were meeting was shaken. And they were all filled with the Holy Spirit and spoke the word of God boldly" (Acts 4:31)*. It almost sounds like a second Pentecost, and this was clearly another outpouring of the Spirit in power and with physical signs. We need the Holy Spirit to be poured into us many times.

In *1 Thessalonians 4:8*, Paul writes about God *"who gives you his Holy Spirit"* and for me this is not just at Baptism and Confirmation, but again and again. The gift will not be forced upon me, however, and if I do not believe in the person and the power of the Holy Spirit and know that God is giving him, I will not ask and so I will not receive either a new sending of this gift of God, or a release of the Spirit already present within me.

Come, Holy Spirit!

Today we pray 'Come, Holy Spirit!' in both formal and informal ways, and this is accepted as perfectly proper and correct. When we pray this prayer, we should expect there to be a new coming of the Holy Spirit to strengthen us for what lies ahead - just as there was when the disciples prayed for a new boldness in *Acts 4:31*.

So today I am of the opinion there is always a new sending of the Spirit when we pray **'Come, Holy Spirit!'** **'Lord, fill me with your Spirit!'** or **'Lord, baptise me in your Holy Spirit!'** But the first time we consciously do this, the grace already given at our Baptism and Confirmation is also released within us, resulting in an explosion of Holy Spirit power in our lives. This is what we call Baptism in the Spirit. The pragmatic side of me simply says "don't worry too much about the explanations, just ask. God will answer and you will know the presence and power of the Holy Spirit in your life - you can deal with the explanations later". This is how theology is supposed to work, anyway. The result can be a sudden and dramatic change accompanied by overwhelming emotions – joy, praise, repentance, tears, love. Or we can experience almost nothing, and only realise something happened when we look back at what has changed over a period of weeks or months.

So I am sure that for those already baptised, there is both a release and a new sending of the Spirit when we ask Jesus to baptise us in his Holy Spirit. I am delighted that some fine theologians are presenting good arguments for the work of the Holy Spirit - this is essential. But sadly their papers will rarely reach the person in the pew, and so for most of us Baptism in the Spirit is a grace that can only be understood by looking for changes in the lives of those who say they have received it. Let's avoid the temptation to concentrate on the how and what of Baptism in the Holy Spirit, and just accept that the prayer of invitation is effective – we ask, he comes. But unless we know that there is a Holy Spirit who wants to come to us, believe in him and know that he will be given, we will never ask, and we will never experience his coming.

A moment of surrender

There has to be a moment of surrender, a moment when we say an unreserved YES to God in a deep and powerful way:

yes to who he is and all that he has done for us;

yes to all that he wants to give us;

yes and welcome to the life-changing, in-dwelling Holy Spirit;

yes to his will, and no to our own selfish desires.

This is Baptism in the Holy Spirit, freely available to all who are willing to step out and say this YES. Through it a full life of faith is no longer just a possibility – it can become a reality. But for many, this amazing gift of the Spirit has been received, but never opened. We need to open the gift.

HOW DO WE DESCRIBE 'BAPTISM IN THE HOLY SPIRIT'?

It is the fulfilment of the promise of the Father:
"...how much more will your Father in heaven give the Holy Spirit to those who ask him!" Luke 11:13

It is the fulfilment of the promise of the Son:
"Unless I go away, the Counsellor will not come to you; but if I go I will send him to you" John 16:7

It results in a closer, transformed relationship with Jesus as Lord:

"No one can say Jesus is Lord except by the Holy Spirit"
1 Corinthians 12:3

It introduces us to God as a loving Father:

"...but you received the Spirit of sonship. And by him we cry 'Abba, Father'. Romans 8:15

It's an experience that makes both Jesus and the Father real to us:

"We proclaim to you what we have seen and heard, so that you also may have fellowship with us. And our fellowship is with the Father and with his Son, Jesus Christ" 1 John 1:3

It results in spontaneous vocal praise and worship of God:

"...we hear them declaring the wonders of God in our own tongues!" Acts 2:11

It makes us more aware of the importance of sacramental Baptism as our new birth in Christ:

"...no-one can enter the Kingdom of God unless he is born of water and the Spirit" John 3:5

It is the provision of power and zeal to serve and to evangelise:

"...and you will be my witnesses..." Acts 1:8. "Evangelisation will never be possible without the Holy Spirit" Evangelii Nuntiandi 75, 1975 Exhortation of Pope Paul VI

It is the entrance into the spiritual gifts for mission and service:

"Now to each is given the manifestation of the Spirit for the

common good" 1 Corinthians 12:4-12 *and Vatican II document 'Lumen Gentium' section 12.*

It promotes a greater awareness of the importance of social justice:

"The Spirit of the Lord is on me, because he has anointed me to preach good news to the poor. He has sent me to proclaim freedom for the prisoners and recovery of sight for the blind, to release the oppressed..." Luke 4:18; *"There were no needy persons among them...* Acts 4:34

It makes us aware of the spiritual battle between the forces of light and darkness:

"For our struggle is... against the powers of this dark world and against the spiritual forces of evil in the heavenly realms" Eph.6:12

It is often a physical experience:

"After they prayed the place where they were meeting was shaken. And they were all filled with the Holy Spirit..." Acts 4:31

It creates that greater unity among Christians for which Jesus prayed:

"May they be brought to complete unity to let the world know that you sent me" John 17:23. "Renewal in the Spirit... is manifesting itself as a substantially similar event in most of the Christian Churches and denominations"; "...it is a very special grace for ecumenism" Ecumenism and Charismatic Renewal 21 and 19, Cardinal Leon-Josef Suenens.

It allows the Spirit to work in us to produce more fruit:

"But the fruit of the Spirit is..." Galatians 5:22-26

It is not a once and for all experience – we must go on being filled with the Holy Spirit:
"...be filled with the Spirit" Ephesians 5:18

It is freely given:
"...how much more will your Father in heaven give the Holy Spirit to those who ask him!" Luke 11:13

Forgive me for repeating - Baptism in the Holy Spirit is not something we earn or merit, and none of the results come about through our own ability. It is a gift from God, freely given to those who ask. It is the presence, love, life, and power of God, freely given to us to renew us both inwardly and outwardly, and to enable us to live a full and effective Christian life. When we ask to be baptised in the Holy Spirit, it is Jesus the baptiser we are seeking - he is the one who baptises us in his Spirit. When he does so, his Holy Spirit does not just provide the supernatural power we need to live our Christian lives, but equally importantly he comes to us as a loving friend and helper to protect and guide us in everything we do. Let us always remember that Jesus and his Spirit are never apart – they are conjoined and inseparable.

It releases Grace:
Baptism in the Spirit is at the same time a release of the restricted graces of our Baptism and Confirmation and a new outpouring of the grace and power of the Holy Spirit. It is available to us at any time in our lives and supplies what has been missing as a result of an inadequate response to our Christian initiation. In a certain way it shows the institutional (sacraments) and charismatic (gifts) dimensions in the life of the Church working together to produce

a powerful and effective result - committed disciples on fire with the Spirit.

Plunged into the Holy Spirit:

To baptise means to plunge into or to immerse in. When we are initiated as Christians and baptised in water, we are plunged into Christ and into his Body, the Church. This deals with Original Sin, is the first step in our salvation, and because we receive Christ we also receive his Spirit. Baptism in the Spirit is when Jesus, as he promised, plunges us into his Holy Spirit – he is the baptiser, the one into whom we are plunged is the Holy Spirit. This is to help us be effective Christians, to equip us to serve. It happens because we ask for it – we are plunged into the life of God himself.

The Promise that we will be baptised in the Holy Spirit occurs in the New Testament, once in each gospel and then in the book of Acts:

"...he (Jesus) will baptise you with the Holy Spirit and with fire."
Matthew 3:11
"...but he (Jesus) will baptise you with the Holy Spirit" Mark 1:8
"He will baptise you with the Holy Spirit and with fire" Luke 3:16
"...is he who will baptise with the Holy Spirit" John 1:33
"...in a few days you will be baptised with the Holy Spirit"
Acts 1:5

As the early church community began to spread the Gospel, we find a number of accounts of new Christians receiving the Holy Spirit, among them are these:

- **Peter on Pentecost Day:** *Acts 2:38-39 "you will receive the gift of the Holy Spirit".*

- Peter and John in Samaria: *Acts 8:14-17 "...and they received the Holy Spirit."*
- Peter with Cornelius: *Acts 10:44-46 "...the Holy Spirit came on all..."*
- Paul in Ephesus: *Acts 19:1-6 "When Paul laid his hands on them, the Holy Spirit came on them, they spoke in tongues and prophesied."*

Some other terms used today instead of Baptism in the Spirit are:

- Renewed in the Spirit; Filled with the Spirit; Released in the Spirit;
- Anointed with the Spirit; Immersed in the Spirit;
- Effusion de l'Esprit; Effusione dello Spirito; Efusion del Espiritu;
- The outpouring of the Spirit; The re-kindling of the Spirit

In the Book of Acts we find that the word FILLED is frequently used:

- On Pentecost Day:
  "All of them were filled with the Holy Spirit..." Acts 2:4.
- Peter before the Sanhedrin:
  "Then Peter, filled with the Holy Spirit, said to them..." Acts 4:8
- At the choosing of the seven deacons:
  "...men who are known to be full of the Spirit and wisdom."
  "They chose Stephen, a man full of faith and of the Holy Spirit" Acts 6:1-6

'Baptised in the Holy Spirit' and 'Filled with the Holy Spirit' are the normal phrases found in the Bible. But the description is not really important, nor is the way in which it happens - we are all individuals, and God deals with us uniquely and personally. What is important is that we receive the fullness of the Spirit – his love, life, and power, making us complete and effective Christians, with God now free to work in and through us.

The Years of Blessing

It is estimated that over 120 million Catholics *(David Barrett – World Christian Encyclopedia, Oxford 2001)* have been Baptised in the Holy Spirit since 1967, and when we add the number from the main-line Protestant churches and include the Pentecostals and the Charismatic Independent or Non-Denominational churches, we find that one third of global Christians will say they have experienced this amazing outpouring of grace, and have been filled with the Holy Spirit. If we look deeper we will discover that this one third is the fastest growing part of the Christian Church worldwide, and at the current rate could represent half of all Christians by 2025. We should be on our knees in thanksgiving, because whatever our spirituality or denomination, we need to take Baptism in the Holy Spirit very seriously indeed. It is not something just for a group of enthusiasts – it's vitally important for all of us if we are to receive the fullness of the Father's gift to his children, and it is offered to everyone who asks for it. Against this background and with all this in mind, we'll move on to our next question.

HOW CAN WE RECEIVE THIS NEW LIFE IN THE HOLY SPIRIT?

We have already looked at this question in chapter two, and we have seen that new life in the Spirit is a gift, but we need to ask for it. Jesus says in John 7:37:

"'If anyone is thirsty, let him come to me and drink. Whoever believes in me, as the Scripture has said, streams of living water will flow from within him'. By this he meant the Spirit, whom those who believed in him were later to receive. Up to that time the Spirit had not been given, since Jesus had not yet been glorified."

Living water is always flowing, bringing life to desert places as the prophets tell us:

"For I will pour water on the thirsty land, and streams on the dry ground; I will pour out my Spirit on your offspring, and my blessing on your descendents" Isaiah 44:3.

And as Jesus explains to the Samaritan woman at Jacob's well:

"...whoever drinks the water I give him will never thirst. Indeed the water I give him will become in him a spring of living water welling up to eternal life" John 4:14.

So we must acknowledge our need, want to receive, and then come to Jesus and ask. We need to believe in him and in the promise, and we may need to deal with doubts, fears, barriers, and obstacles that stand in the way. It will certainly be important to repent of our sins, and to want to be right with God *Acts 2:38-39*, but this does not mean we have to be perfect or we would be waiting forever. When the Spirit comes in power he will convict us of sin *John 16:8*. Repentance will usually be the doorway to receiving the fullness of the Spirit, but sometimes it follows filling with the Holy Spirit, because until then we may not be able to see the areas in our lives where we need to change.

Many just don't see the need to repent, and this can be the biggest obstacle between us and God, but the Spirit will show us our sin. God deals with us step by step – if he revealed to us all that needed to change in one moment, we might give up before we even begin. The Christian life is a journey of discovery.

Let me repeat those key words:
Need – Want – Come – Ask – Repent - Receive

Jesus can baptise us in his Holy Spirit at any time and in any place. We may be alone or in a crowd; often we will be with others who have already received this new life, and they will lay hands on us *(Acts 8:17; 19:5-6)* and pray with us. We may have decided we need to open our lives to the Holy Spirit, and so followed a course of teaching similar to this one, or we may spontaneously choose to ask Jesus to baptise us in the Spirit without any formal teaching. God is sovereign and deals with us as individuals – no two people have the same experience of the Spirit at work in them. How and when are not the most important thing – what matters is that it happens.

ARE THERE ANY HINDRANCES TO RECEIVING THIS NEW LIFE IN THE HOLY SPIRIT?

Yes, there are, and I will very briefly highlight some of them:

Sin:

- We need to repent of any major sin in our lives of which we are aware.
- We should be clean vessels for the Lord to fill with his Spirit.
- Often we don't see the need for repentance, but God will show us if we ask.
- It may happen that we only become aware of some areas of sin after we have been filled with the Spirit.

Ignorance:

- Some may think that Baptism in the Spirit is a shortcut to holiness. This is not the case, but because we have the Holy Spirit alive in us in a new way, he will help us enter into the holiness that is God's gift to us.
- Nor is Baptism in the Spirit a spiritual status symbol denoting a super-Christian. In fact it reveals how much work remains to be done in us.
- It may wrongly be seen as a goal, whereas it is just a new beginning in our exciting journey of faith – there's always more. It may be regarded as something to solve all our problems, whereas in fact it will highlight them. But the good news is that the Spirit will now equip us to address them - it takes courage to face the truth about ourselves.

Wrong motives:

• Some may seek Baptism in the Spirit for their own reasons. We must accept God's priorities, and these have as their focus witness, evangelisation, service and ministry to others.

• The Spirit is not given to show how wonderful you and I are, but to show everyone how great Jesus is, as Watchman Nee explains it in **'The Normal Christian Life'**, Victory Press, Eastbourne 1964.

Fear:

• We may be afraid of what will happen to us, what God will ask of us, where he will take us. So we need to remember that this is a gift from God to his children – it will help us and be good for us. But it takes courage to change, staying as we are usually feels more comfortable.

• Or we may be afraid of what others will think or say – we need to trust God and not allow human respect to control us. But it takes courage to stand for our new convictions when we know they'll be challenged.

Pride:

• I have often heard remarks like – "Why do I need this? I've been a good Catholic all my life". We may genuinely think we have all we need, but this is a form of pride and it makes us unteachable.

• Often we feel a need to be in control; this is pride and needs to be surrendered.

• We may be proud of our secular mindset and unwilling to surrender it. This has to change.

Resentment:

- There may be things that have happened in our lives which have caused major resentment towards a person or a group of people to build up in us.
- Perhaps we feel we have been wronged, and there may even be some justification for this view, but our unwillingness to forgive will block the working of the Holy Spirit in us.
- To forgive someone is a decision we make even if when we don't 'feel' like forgiving them, and by surrendering our resentment we are released to receive more of the Holy Spirit.

Works:

- Many of us still think we have to somehow earn or deserve God's favour, to be worthy of it. But this discounts God's grace, his desire to freely give us something we cannot deserve or earn. All we must do is believe, come, ask.

Unworthiness:

- Yes, but amazingly to God we are of enormous value – sinners for whom he gave his only Son, lost sheep for whom he searches. Jesus made us worthy.

Unbelief:

- A vague hope dishonours God. We need to confess our lack of faith, and put our full trust in Jesus – this takes courage.
- On October 21st 2009, Pope Benedict expressed it in these words: **"Faith is, above all, a personal intimate encounter with Jesus, to experience his closeness, his friendship, his love; only in this way does one learn to know him more and to love and follow him ever more. May this happen to each**

one of us."
WHAT IS LIKELY TO HAPPEN AFTER WE HAVE RECEIVED THIS GIFT FROM GOD?

Because God deals with everyone as an individual, no one can give a universal answer, but some positive things are likely to happen and some traps must be avoided.

Prayer:
- When someone experiences a new outpouring of the Holy Spirit, it's certain that they will want to pray more and will discover that the Spirit helps them to pray. *"We do not know what we ought to pray for, but the Spirit himself intercedes for us..." Romans 8:26.*

Scripture:
- There will be a new interest in the Bible, a desire to read it, and a better understanding of what is read – Scripture will come alive in a new way.

- This is often accompanied by a willingness to be subject to God's Word:
"All Scripture is God–breathed, and is useful for teaching, rebuking, correcting and training in righteousness, so that the man of God may be thoroughly equipped for every good work" 2 Timothy 3:16-17.

- In the 2003 papal document **'Ecclesia in Europa', 65, Pope John Paul II** wrote:

"May the Holy Bible continue to be a treasure for the Church and for every Christian... Let us take up this book! Let us receive it from the Lord who continually offers it to us through his Church. Let us devour it (cf Revelation 10:9) so that it can become our very life... Filled with hope, we will be able to share it with every man and woman we encounter on our way".

Sacraments:

• The sacraments will become more important, especially the Eucharist and the Sacrament of Reconciliation.
"For whenever you eat this bread and drink this cup, you proclaim the Lord's death until he comes" 1 Cor.11:26
"We implore you on Christ's behalf; be reconciled to God" 2 Cor.5:20

• Also in 'Ecclesia in Europa' 74, Pope John Paul II wrote:
"A prominent place needs to be given to the celebration of the sacraments... In the knowledge that in them Christ himself is acting through the Holy Spirit..."

Personal Holiness:

• There will be a new desire to live a holy life in the power of the Spirit.
"Now you have been set free from sin and have become slaves to God, the benefit you reap leads to holiness and the result is eternal life" Rom.6:22

Joy, Praise and worship:

• When the Spirit is alive in us, it is entirely natural that we will have a greater joy and desire to thank, praise, and worship God, both publicly and privately.

"Is anyone happy? Let him sing songs of praise" James 5:13.

The Second Coming:

- A new interest in Christ's Second Coming is often aroused:

2 Cor. 5: 4-5 "For while we are in this tent, we groan and are burdened, because we do not wish to be unclothed but to be clothed with our heavenly dwelling, so that what is mortal may be swallowed up by life. Now it is God who has made us for this very purpose and has given us the Spirit as a deposit, guaranteeing what is to come."

Love for God and our neighbour; a desire for community:

- The first result of a new release of the Holy Spirit will always be an increase in love. We will be filled with the love of God the Father and of his son, Jesus Christ. Our hearts of stone are broken and replaced with hearts of flesh, and this experience of God's love will affect all our relationships *Ezekiel 36:26.*

- Most people find they have a greater love for God and for others. It is surprising to discover a new love for people we were not previously drawn to.

- This leads to a desire to be more involved in the local church or community, and to seek fellowship with those who share the same experience of the Spirit.

- There will be a new desire for justice, a willingness to help those in trouble. *Acts 2:42-47* encapsulates what resulted when the Spirit came in power:

"They devoted themselves to the apostles' teaching and to the fellowship, to the breaking of bread and to prayer. Everyone was filled with awe and many wonders and miraculous signs were done by the apostles. All the believers were together and had

everything in common. Selling their possessions and goods they gave to anyone as he had need. Every day they continued to meet together in the temple courts. They broke bread in their homes and ate together with glad and sincere hearts, praising God and enjoying the favour of all the people. And the Lord added daily to their number those who were being saved".

There are no reasons why we should not expect very similar results when the Holy Spirit is free to work in us. Wouldn't it be wonderful if the above Scripture verses described life in our parishes today? But the greatest, the most essential and life-changing result of Baptism in the Holy Spirit, is the realisation that Jesus is Lord: *No-one can say "Jesus is Lord" except by the Holy Spirit (I Corinthians 12:3).*

There are also some pitfalls to be avoided:

Pride – again!
- No one is better than another, but God is gracious to all who seek him and ask.
- To avoid the dangers of spiritual pride, it is helpful to take on new areas of service in the church, or to carry out the more difficult and unpopular tasks. *"I hate pride and arrogance..."* *Proverbs 8:13*

Criticism:
- There is a danger of feeling superior to those who have not received a new outpouring of the Spirit.
- This may result in criticising what we see as their limited vision and expectation of God.

"For in the same way you judge others, you will be judged"

Matthew 7:1

Cooling off:
• We cannot expect to stay at the top of the mountain, but we must be careful not to lose our enthusiasm. We need to stay close to the Lord – *"I am the vine, you are the branches..." John 15:5.*

Seeking experiences:
• Some go from place to place in search of the latest experience or novelty. Paul describes this in *2 Timothy 4:3 "...they will gather around them a great number of teachers to say what their itching ears want to hear."*
• The challenge is to get involved in normal, everyday life, bringing Christ more and more into our homes, our places of work and leisure, and our parishes.

When we experience new life in the Spirit, we may spend time in the wilderness, just like Jesus did: *"Jesus... was led by the Spirit into the desert..." Luke 4: 1-13.* This is to test us, and will make us stronger in our faith. Temptations will come, but we are equipped to deal with them and they should not discourage us. But whilst we are in a new place spiritually, it's only the beginning, and we need to learn how to walk in the love and power of God's Holy Spirit. As Paul told the Galatian Christians: *"Since we live by the Spirit, let us keep in step with the Spirit. Let us not become conceited, provoking, envying each other" Gal 5:25-26.*

Come, claim the Promise!
To sum up: Baptism in the Holy Spirit is the fulfilment of the promise of the Father, released to us by the work of Jesus. It is a free gift, given to those who are thirsty and ask. So we must come

thirsty, repentant, obedient, and full of faith - to claim the promise requires a definite act of faith. We may face all sorts of doubts and questions – what will happen, will it work, what will others think, will I have to change?

Or perhaps we think it seems too easy, too good to be true? But God has promised, so we come to claim his promise and to receive his gift of new life in the Spirit. He will not disappoint us – he will give a new colour and a new definition to everything around us. It's good to keep in mind that the most important evidence of Baptism in the Holy Spirit is not miraculous signs, but this new revelation of the person of Jesus Christ. We see him in a new way, our response is "Oh, yes, Lord!" and something in us changes.

Stanley Jebb, a Baptist minister, once expressed it like this:
"The Baptism in the Spirit provides power in witness, a new ability in prayer, an entrance into the realm of spiritual gifts and a willingness to suffer for Christ. None of these things come through our own ability. All depend on the enabling grace of God through his Holy Spirit. One of the loveliest results of this experience is a deeper love for the Lord and for one another, and the coming of the Holy Spirit results in greater unity among believers".

Pope Benedict XVI
On Pentecost Sunday, May 11th 2008, Pope Benedict XVI publicly challenged us to rediscover what it means to be baptised in the Holy Spirit:

"Today I would like to extend this invitation to everyone: let us rediscover, dear brothers and sisters, the beauty of being baptised

in the Holy Spirit; let us be aware again of our Baptism and Confirmation, sources of grace that are always present."

For Pope Benedict, Pentecost Day is **"the crowning moment of Jesus' whole mission"**, fulfilling the prophecy of John the Baptist *"He (Jesus) will baptise you in the Holy Spirit" Matthew 3:11. "Then the Spirit of God was poured out in a super-abundant way, like a waterfall able to purify every heart, to extinguish the flames of evil and ignite the fire of divine love in the world".*

Earlier, in his Angelus message on the feast of the Baptism of the Lord, January 13th 2008, the Pope had spoken these words: *"Jesus was revealed as the One who came to baptise humanity in the Holy Spirit; he came to give men and women life in abundance" (see John 10:10).*

These statements by Pope Benedict help us to understand the link between our sacramental Baptism and Baptism in the Holy Spirit. We are expected to experience the Spirit in a **super-abundant** way, like a **waterfall** purifying our hearts, destroying evil, and igniting the fire of God's love. Baptism in the Spirit is when we open our lives to this powerful waterfall of the Holy Spirit, which brings us life to the full, *John 10:10*.

With all this on offer, who can possibly hold back?

Praying for Baptism in the Holy Spirit

There is not really a right and a wrong way to pray for Baptism in the Holy Spirit - God is Sovereign and will act as he chooses, as we know from examples in the Book of Acts (Acts 10:44-48). But there are some factors to consider and it's worth looking at these.

Anyone may receive prayer for Baptism in the Holy Spirit at any time and in any place, but it is more effective when a person is seeking it for the right reasons and has understood that they should prepare for it spiritually. This has already been explained earlier in the chapter. Probably the most common way to approach Baptism in the Holy Spirit is by following a course of six or seven sessions, usually described as a Life in the Spirit Seminar, which clearly presents the basic Christian teaching on God's Love, Salvation, the Gift of the Holy Spirit, Receiving the New Life the Spirit brings, the prayer for Baptism in the Holy Spirit, and concluding with Growing in the Transforming Life of the Spirit. Such a course is often offered by parishes, communities, prayer groups or similar, will include talks, small group sharing and discussion, and will give ample opportunity for personal questions and clarifications.

The actual prayer for Baptism in the Holy Spirit will often be offered by the leaders of the seminars and the small groups, and will consist of an invitation to Jesus to pour out his Holy Spirit upon the candidate and into his or her life in a new way, and to release the power of the Spirit already present in the person if they have been baptised. The prayer will normally be accompanied by the laying on of hands (Acts 8:17) and with an expectation that with this new outpouring of the Spirit will come one or more of the supernatural gifts listed in 1 Corinthians 12 and dealt with in the next chapter of this book. These are gifts not rights; they require an openness on the part of the person being prayed with, and will be given according to the will of God and not the person's request. The results to be expected after the prayer are looked at in the following chapters.

To live a fuller life in the Holy Spirit means turning from ourselves and our plans and desires, to God and his purposes and equipping for our lives. This means listening every day to the voice and guidance of the Holy Spirit and doing everything in his strength, not in our own, and giving the power, the control and the glory back to God.

In Rome, on June 1st 2014, Pope Francis addressed a large gathering of Italian Charismatic Catholics who would testify to their experience of the life-changing power of the Holy Spirit, and told them: 'I expect from you that you share with all in the Church the grace of Baptism in the Spirit...'

So may I encourage every reader to ask prayer for this blessing, confident that the Lord will respond to our invitation:

Come, Holy Spirit!

Discuss the following statements
with reference to the Scriptures:

Being Baptised in the Spirit is the fulfilment
of the promise of the Father, and his gift
to every Christian who asks for it

We can all receive this gift and enter fully
into the new life in the Spirit

There may be hindrances and
objections to be dealt with

Things will be different afterwards –
we will experience much that is positive,
but there are also some pitfalls to be avoided

The Scriptures:

John 7:37-39 and Luke 11: 1-13

The Questions:

Do you really know what it means when you
hear the phrase 'baptised in the Holy Spirit?'
How would you explain it?

CHAPTER FOUR

THE GIFTS OF THE HOLY SPIRIT

- **What are these special gifts or charisms, and to whom are they given?**
- **Which particular gifts of the Holy Spirit are we talking about?**

An Introduction to Charisms

Where does this word 'charism' come from, and what exactly does it mean? The root is found in the Greek word 'charis' meaning grace, and 'charisma' meaning a work of grace or a gift of grace. Every charism is a special gift of grace because it is supernaturally given by an intervention of the Holy Spirit to equip a person to undertake a particular task or service for the benefit of the Church. This teaching of St. Paul is fully endorsed in section 12 of Lumen Gentium, the Second Vatican Council's important document on the nature of the Church: **"Allotting his gifts as he wills, he also distributes special graces among the faithful of every rank"**. In the view of St. Paul, the charisms show the particular function we have in the Christian community, where there will be a rich variety of charisms in operation.

Charisms are not for our personal sanctification, but are given for the benefit of the community.

"Each one should use whatever gift he has received to serve others, faithfully administering God's grace in its various forms" I Peter 4:10.

"We have different gifts according to the grace given us. If a man's gift is prophesying, let him use it... If it is serving, let him serve; if it is teaching, let him teach..." Romans 12:6-8.

1 Corinthians 12

When we search the Scriptures, we find examples of many gifts and ministries given by the Holy Spirit, but for the purposes of our study I will be concentrating on the list of charisms or special graces referred to by St. Paul in chapter 12 of his first letter to the Corinthians. Here he was not giving an introduction to the charisms - he was clearly writing to a community that was already familiar with the charisms, but was misusing these gifts of the Holy Spirit. So to fully appreciate his teaching we really need to study chapters 13 and 14 as well, since these chapters deal with the climate in which the gifts are to be used and emphasize the importance of always making sure there is good order. For our purposes, however, we first need to examine his list of gifts in chapter 12 in some detail, consider why we need them in today's advanced and sophisticated world, and then take a more general look at how we are to use them.

Dealing with ignorance

"Now about spiritual gifts, brothers, I do not want you to be ignorant" 1 Cor.12:1.

Paul's opening sentence makes it clear that when it came to the spiritual gifts or charisms, there was ignorance in this early Christian community.

Things have not changed much – there is still a lot of ignorance today, and many people know nothing about the spiritual gifts, not even that they exist. The difference, however, is that in the church of Corinth there was an excessive use of some of the gifts causing disorder in their meetings, whereas today there is a lack of use of the gifts in our churches. We are missing something important. Today some believe the charismatic gifts were given to the early church but have since been withdrawn (a cessationist view), whilst others think they are now only given in exceptional circumstances to very holy and specially chosen people - Saints. Neither of these views is correct, nor is the view that came into the Church during the Age of Enlightenment, when people began to believe they could explain everything using their reason. There was a fear of the supernatural, so because they couldn't explain the spiritual gifts, they simply dismissed them as of no importance. None of these views conform to Scripture and the teaching of the Church today, expressed in the Catholic Catechism sections 798 - 801.

Vatican Council II and Church teaching

At the second session of the Second Vatican Council in October 1963, there was a debate about the spiritual gifts. The debate centred on whether in our day the charisms are given to many of the faithful so that they can help to build up the Church, or whether such gifts are extremely rare and exceptional. The view that prevailed was that it is not only through the sacraments and official ministries that the Holy Spirit equips and leads the Church, but that the charisms are special graces which are also essential for the life of the Church. The Holy Spirit still distributes them among the faithful of every rank, and they are to be received with gratitude and used for the renewal and building up of the Church.

As a result of the debate about the charisms, we find this teaching in **Lumen Gentium 12**, the Second Vatican Council's document on the Church:

"**It is not only through the sacraments and Church ministries that the Holy Spirit makes holy the People of God, leads them and enriches them with his virtues. Allotting his gifts as he wills (1 Cor.12:11), he also distributes special graces among the faithful of every rank. By these gifts he makes them fit and ready to undertake various tasks and offices for the renewal and building up of the Church**".

"**Whether these charisms be very remarkable or more simple and widely diffused, they are to be received with thanksgiving and consolation, since they are fitting and useful for the needs of the Church**" (Lumen Gentium section 12).

This teaching is very clearly based on the teaching of St. Paul, particularly in *1 Corinthians 12*, which we will be examining in more detail.

Pope John Paul II and the charismatic dimension of the Church

At the special meeting with **The Ecclesial Movements and the New Communities** on the eve of Pentecost, May 30th 1998, which took place outside St. Peter's, Rome, Pope John Paul II said:

"**The Spirit is always awesome whenever he intervenes. He arouses astonishing new events, he radically changes people and history. This was the unforgettable experience of the Second Vatican Council, during which, guided by the same Spirit, the**

Church rediscovered the charismatic dimension as being essential to her identity. The institutional and charismatic aspects are co-essential to the configuration of the Church, and they co-operate, although in different ways, towards its life, its renewal, and the sanctification of the People of God. It is from this providential rediscovery of the Church's charismatic dimension that, before and after the Council, there has been a remarkable development of ecclesial movements and new communities."

In the **Catechism of the Catholic Church section 800** we find that:
"**Charisms are to be accepted with gratitude by the person who receives them, and by all members of the Church as well. They are a wonderfully rich grace for the apostolic vitality and for the holiness of the entire Body of Christ, provided they are really genuine gifts of the Holy Spirit and are used in full conformity with authentic promptings of this same Spirit, that is, in keeping with charity, the true measure of all charisms.**"

Then in **section 2003** we are told that:
"**Whatever their character – sometimes it is extraordinary, as the gift of miracles or of tongues – charisms are oriented toward sanctifying grace, and are intended for the common good of the Church. They are at the service of charity which builds up the Church.**"

Why do we need doctrine and teaching when we have the Spirit and his gifts?

A good way to explain why we need doctrine and teaching as well as the Holy Spirit is the illustration of a sailing boat, which I believe originated with Donald Gee, a well-known Pentecostal leader. In addition to its sail, a sailing boat needs quite a heavy keel to give it balance. Without a sail it will go nowhere, but without the keel the boat is unbalanced and will tip over. We need the wind of the Spirit to fill our sails and move us forward, but we also need the heavy keel to keep us upright. There is no conflict between doctrine and Spirit, teaching and experience, institutional and charismatic – just a healthy balance. Both are necessary.

Institutional and Charismatic

Pope John Paul II reminded us that the institutional and charismatic dimensions of the Church are both essential to her life. The institutional and structural dimension has been passed down from generation to generation since the time of the Apostles, whereas the charismatic dimension bursts into the life of the Church in unexpected ways. The institution needs the charismatic dimension to bring the life of the Spirit into the structures, to the people, and to give vision, whilst the charismatic needs the institution to discern and guide it, to protect it and ensure it is accepted and nurtured. It also needs the discernment of the Church authorities to protect it from error. It has always been the case that the office of Apostle is in the first place among the ministries and gifts, and that authority in the Church is therefore vested in the Apostles and their successors, the bishops. In *Acts 15:2* Paul and Barnabas report the miraculous signs and wonders they have seen among the Gentiles to the Council of Jerusalem, fully prepared to accept the decision of James and the Council members on the question of circumcision of the Gentile converts. In the same way today, those Catholics who have experienced Baptism in the Spirit fully accept the authority of the Pope and the hierarchy, and look to them for discernment, guidance and support in all matters concerning life in the Spirit and the charismatic gifts. The attitudes and understanding of Popes Paul VI, John Paul II, and Benedict XVI have played a vital role in ensuring that the Church has accepted the new movements and communities, encouraging them to take their place in the life of the Church. The popes understood that the charismatic gifts are not given for personal benefit, nor are they spiritual trophies to show how special the recipients are. They are given to equip, enable, and empower the Church as it reaches out to serve the needy world around it and to bring the Gospel to everyone. The charisms show God in action, and they will be given when we find ourselves in situations where they are needed.

The Confirmation gifts - Isaiah 11:2

Here in Isaiah we find reference made to *"the Spirit of wisdom and of understanding, the Spirit of counsel and of power, the Spirit of knowledge and of fear of the Lord"*. When I was confirmed I was taught that I would receive these gifts of the Spirit for my personal growth, and that they would be given to everyone who received a new outpouring of the Holy Spirit in the Sacrament of Confirmation. So they are not the charismatic gifts of grace we are discussing in this chapter, but they are still valid and genuine gifts of the Spirit given for a different purpose (Catechism 1831). The weakness at my Confirmation was that these were the only gifts I heard about. Against this background, let's look at our questions on the charismatic gifts.

WHAT ARE THE SPIRITUAL GIFTS OR CHARISMS AND TO WHOM ARE THEY GIVEN?

They are different supernatural gifts of grace given to us by the Holy Spirit, to enrich the lives of those around us:

"There are different kinds of gifts, but the same Spirit. There are different kinds of service, but the same Lord. There are different kinds of working, but the same God works all of them in all men" **1 Corinthians 12:4-6.**

Every charism is a gift – but not every gift is a charism

As we have already seen, the word 'charism' means "a special gift of grace" (**Catholic Catechism 799**). It is special because it has a supernatural dimension to it, so it is not the same as a natural talent - which is also a gift from God – but it may add a new dimension to a natural ability. The charisms are the various ways in which special gifts of grace are evident in the lives of individual men and women, making them powerful channels of grace to others in the Christian community and beyond. A charism is a special gift because it is freely given to us, but it belongs to God and not to us. In a certain sense he 'lends' a gift to us for a specific occasion and purpose - our task is to receive it, and use it as the Spirit leads us: *"Now to each one the manifestation of the Spirit is given for the common good"* **1 Corinthians 12:7.**

Gifts from a Loving Father

There is, therefore, no reason for us to be ignorant or afraid – we need to embrace the teaching of Scripture, clearly interpreted by the Church, and be open to the gifts of the Holy Spirit in our own lives, ready to receive them and use them. We are all members of the one body *(1 Cor. 12:12-31)*, and we are to use the gifts the Spirit gives us. If we do not, others are impoverished, because these gifts are not for our personal benefit but for the good and the benefit of those around us. If we are open, God will use us as channels for his gifts so that his life-changing power can reach others. In the teaching of Paul, the body of Christ is extremely important. It is the visible church, a community made up of a variety of people with a variety of functions and gifts. It's important to remember that they are gifts, freely given to us according to the sovereign will and purpose of God. They are not prizes, or rewards given for particular merit, so they are not something earned or deserved by special people. God is showing that he is a loving Father, and wants to give good gifts that will meet the needs of all his children through ordinary faithful members of his body, not only through ordained ministers.

The gifts are:

Spiritual	(pneumatika)	- not talents, but special gifts of the Holy Spirit
Gifts	(charismata)	- not prizes, but freely given as God chooses
Services	(diakoniai)	- to serve others, not ourselves
Powers	(energemata)	- momentary powers, not permanent possessions
Manifestations	(phanerosa)	- visible acts, showing God's presence

We can summarise the above by saying that they are spiritual powers above our natural abilities, freely given to us by the Holy Spirit, to be used for the benefit of others, and producing definite, often visible, results. All of us are encouraged to *"eagerly desire spiritual gifts" 1 Cor. 14:1*, but then we must leave it to the Holy Spirit to give them to those he wishes, knowing that he gives us different gifts *"and he gives them to each one just as he determines" 1 Cor.12:11.* We may desire a particular gift and ask God for it, but it may not be the one he wants to give us. It is his decision, and we must accept his will.

SO WHICH PARTICULAR GIFTS OF THE HOLY SPIRIT ARE WE TALKING ABOUT?

We believe we are created by God, and that he is the source of all that we have and are. So every good gift comes from him, and this includes our natural abilities and talents as well as the special gifts of grace or charisms he may give us through the Holy Spirit. But here we are still talking about charisms – not about natural abilities. We find a number of gifts and ministries listed in the writings of Paul – let me refer to *Ephesians 4:11-12:*

"It was he who gave some to be apostles, some to be prophets, some to be evangelists, and some to be pastors and teachers, to prepare God's people for works of service, so that the body of Christ may be built up..."

Then in *Romans 12:6-8* we find this list:

"We have different gifts according to the grace given us. If a man's gift is prophesying, let him use it in proportion to his faith. If it is serving, let him serve; if it is teaching, let him teach; if it is encouraging, let him encourage; if it is contributing to the needs of others, let him give generously; if it is leadership, let him govern diligently; if it is showing mercy, let him do it cheerfully."

All these gifts are important for building up the body of Christ, but in these two scriptures Paul is mainly writing about gifts that supernaturally equip people for their particular vocations or callings. Apostles, prophets, teachers, evangelists, and leaders are important ministries that will have a profound effect on the way those called to them live their lives. Encouraging, giving generously, showing mercy - these are gifts that are more widely distributed in the body. When it comes to the main offices in the church, charisms both demonstrate the particular function each person has, and equip the person to perform that function.

The most discussed list of charisms: 1 Corinthians 12:7-10

Having recognised that God gives many gifts, our focus here is on the list of gifts or charisms from *1 Corinthians chapter 12*. Here in verses *7-10* we find the gifts listed. Right from the beginning, Paul makes it absolutely clear that the gifts of the Spirit are given for the good of everyone. He then goes on to list the particular gifts he has in mind:

"Now to each one the manifestation of the Spirit is given for the common good. To one there is given through the Spirit the message of wisdom, to another the message of knowledge by means of the same Spirit, to another faith by the same Spirit, to another gifts of healing by that one Spirit, to another miraculous powers, to another prophecy, to another distinguishing between spirits, to another speaking in different kinds of tongues, and to still another the interpretation of tongues. All these are the work of one and the same Spirit, and he gives them to each one, just as he determines".

One way to consider these gifts is to divide them into three groups. The divisions are rather artificial, and gifts from different groups are sometimes used together, but I find it a helpful way of approaching them.

Group One contains what may be called the 'knowing' or 'revelation' gifts:
- the message of wisdom
- the message of knowledge
- the distinguishing between spirits

Group Two are the 'doing' or 'power' gifts:
- the gift of faith
- gifts of healing
- miraculous powers

Group Three is made up of the 'speaking' or 'inspiration' gifts:
- prophecy

- different kinds of tongues
- the interpretation of tongues

Each of these gifts involves a supernatural manifestation of the power of God. In one sense everything God does is supernatural, that is his nature, but here we are looking at actual demonstrations of his presence and power, so let's consider each of them.

Group one – the 'knowing' or 'revelation' gifts:

1. The message of wisdom:
The message of wisdom is a revelation given by the Holy Spirit, of something known only to God. It will often point to the future, to something in the purpose or plan of God, and will address the needs of a person or situation. It may come to us through a vision, a dream, an inner conviction, perhaps through prophecy, or a message in tongues with an interpretation. The message of wisdom has nothing to do with our intellectual capacity, nor is it linked to the sort of worldly wisdom that enables us to deal with the affairs of life or to give wise counsel. It applies God's wisdom to a particular situation in a way that is beyond our natural ability.

An example from the Book of Acts is Peter's vision of the unclean food he was instructed to eat, and his subsequent journey to the house of the Gentile Cornelius in *Acts 10:9-48.* God gives Peter a vision which reveals something totally contrary to the way Peter understands the law. Firstly eating food that is ritually unclean, then giving hospitality to Gentiles, entering the house of a Gentile, and finally preaching the Gospel to the Gentiles - none of which would be accepted by a good Jew. So God prepares him in a vision for what is going to happen, knowing it is completely outside Peter's way of thinking. Through this miraculous revelation of his will and his plan, God prepares Peter for what he will shortly be facing.

2. The message of knowledge:

This is very similar to the message of wisdom, in that it too is a supernatural revelation given by the Holy Spirit, of something in the mind of God. It usually relates to the present or the past rather than to the future.

God has all knowledge, he is omniscient, but he does not reveal everything to us. Sometimes he just reveals a simple fact, or perhaps just a word, because this is enough to uncover the truth, to open a door, or to point to a solution. Again it is not something we have learned intellectually, or the result of a special study, but something God reveals to us at a particular moment. It is neither a human ability nor a psychic experience.

An example in the New Testament is the meeting of Jesus and the Samaritan women at the well of Sychar, in *John chapter 4*. In *verse 18* Jesus tells her she has had five husbands – knowledge given to him by the Holy Spirit. As a result she sees Jesus as a prophet, and listens even more intently to what he has to say. Similarly, in *Acts 5:3*, Peter knows by the Holy Spirit that Ananias and Sapphira have lied and kept back some of their money instead of giving all of it to the apostles for distribution to those in need. This message of knowledge has a very dramatic effect when he announces it!

The message of knowledge, the message of wisdom, and prophetic insights, may often operate together. Whilst they are distinct gifts, we must avoid worrying about exactly which gift is being given, and follow the prompting of the Spirit. All three of them convey to us, through the power of the Holy Spirit, something God wants us to know for the benefit of one person, of a group, or sometimes of many people – even a whole community.

3. The distinguishing between spirits:

This is a gift involving supernatural insight into the world of all spirits – the Holy Spirit, demons, satanic spirits, and the human spirit. It is the supernatural ability to distinguish the good or evil tendencies in a spirit, or the good or evil power behind a spiritual manifestation. It is not thought-reading, psychological insight, or any kind of mind game, and it is limited to a single group of beings – spirits. Even without the gift of distinguishing between spirits, we may often have an inner witness when something is not of God, particularly if we know his Word and are walking closely with him. But this supernatural gift enables us to recognise with certainty when a spirit is at work, and to react to the situation as the Holy Spirit directs.

In *Ephesians chapter 6 verse 12* St. Paul reminds us that:

"...our struggle is not against flesh and blood, but against the rulers, against the authorities, against the powers of this dark world and against the spiritual forces of evil in the heavenly realms".

It is in this struggle that the spiritual gift of distinguishing or discerning of spirits is of such importance. At a **General Audience in Rome on 15th November 1972, Pope Paul VI** said:

"Evil is not merely a lack of something, but an effective agent, a living spiritual being, perverted and perverting, a terrible reality. It is contrary to the teaching of the Bible and the Church to refuse

to recognise the existence of such a reality or to explain it as a pseudo-reality, a conceptual and fanciful personification of the unknown causes of our misfortunes.

That it is not a question of one devil, but of many, is indicated by various passages in the gospel *(Luke 11:21; Mark 5:9)*. But the principal one is Satan, which means the adversary, the enemy; and with him many, all creatures of God, but fallen because of their rebellion and damnation. The question of the Devil and the influence he can exert on individual persons as well as on communities, whole societies, or events, is a very important chapter of Catholic doctrine which is given little attention today, though it should be studied again."

In his first letter John reminds us in chapter 4 verse 1 "...do not believe every spirit, but test the spirits to see whether they are from God..."

In *Acts 16:16* we find a slave girl, who was possessed by an evil spirit and told fortunes. She follows Paul, Luke and Silas, shouting *"These men are servants of the Most High God who are telling you the way to be saved!"* In the light of Paul's teaching in Ephesians 6, we can see how important it is to be protected against the deceptions of evil spirits by the gift of distinguishing between spirits, particularly as they sometimes masquerade as angels of light – as in the example above where the spirit in the girl actually speaks the truth, they *are* servants of the Most High God, and they *are* telling people about salvation in Jesus. But Paul recognises the presence of a false spirit and acts accordingly, saying to the spirit: *"In the name of Jesus Christ I command you to come out of her! At that moment the spirit left her"(verse 18).*

This gift is the supernatural ability to know what is motivating a person to say or do something. There are three likely sources of this motivation: God the Holy Spirit; a demonic spirit; the human spirit. The way the gift works is that we receive a really strong conviction that God is at work when something is said or done, or that it is not God at all but another spirit of some kind. Often it is just human thinking being expressed, which may be right or wrong, but sometimes there is clearly an evil spirit at work in a person, and they need to be set free from it. This will happen through a prayer of deliverance, or in extreme cases of possession, through a formal exorcism.

Group Two: the 'doing' or 'power' gifts:

4. The gift of Faith:
This gift of faith is given so that we can receive miracles. It is a total conviction that God is going to act in a supernatural way in a particular situation, and that we need to speak or act in order to release his power. We have complete faith that what we are saying or doing is God's will, that he will honour our word or action, and he will make it happen. So it is quite different from the faith that brings us into relationship with God, believing in him and his plan of salvation. Nor is it the simple faith we exercise when we ask God to answer our prayers, and it has nothing to do with faithfulness, which grows in us as a fruit of the presence of the Holy Spirit. Hebrews 11:1 reminds us *"Now faith is being sure of what we hope for and certain of what we do not see."* This gift makes us certain about something we cannot yet see.

Elijah's challenge to the prophets of Baal on Mount Carmel is an amazing example of this gift of faith in action. God gave Elijah the absolutely certainty that he would work a remarkable miracle, but first Elijah had to act *1 Kings 20*.

So with complete faith in God, he sets the scene, issues the challenge, and then plays his part in the total destruction of God's enemies. The key point is that Elijah had to step out in faith and issue the challenge in order that God might be vindicated.

5. Gifts of healing:

What we are dealing with here is the supernatural curing of physical, psychological and emotional diseases - God intervening and bringing healing to a sick person. The original texts use the nouns in the plural because there are many different types of healing needed. The healings come from God, but are channelled through a person who prays or asks for the healing. Throughout the history of the Church there have been healings in answer to prayer, and this is an important part of Catholic Tradition. These gifts of healings are not medical treatments of any sort, but direct interventions by the Holy Spirit. In the letter of *James, chapter 5 verses 14-15,* we read:

"Is any one of you sick? He should call the elders of the church to pray over him and anoint him with oil in the name of the Lord. And the prayer offered in faith will make the sick person well; the Lord will raise him up".

This is what we are all called to do, and while we may not understand why the Lord heals some people and not others, we do know that sometimes through prayer or a word of command, a person is amazingly healed, and we describe this as a gift of healing. As healing can be controversial, I will deal with this gift in more detail.

Paul never describes people as 'healers', because no-one possesses a habitual gift of healing, but there are people who receive a special charism for healing. This doesn't mean they possess the ability to heal whenever they want to, but they are often used by God as channels for his healing power. Every single healing is a gift from God, as each one is an individual encounter with the Lord of love and power. In the four Gospels there are 41 specific instances of healings, and 727 verses (about a fifth of the Gospels) are devoted to the subject of healings. Why did Jesus give so much emphasis to healing? When Jesus heals it's a sign that the Kingdom of God is present, and his purpose is not only to restore us to health and wholeness, but to bring us into this Kingdom where God reigns. Healings reinforced his message of salvation and forgiveness, and he passed this ministry on to his followers, giving his disciples authority to heal in his name in *Matthew 10:1: "He called his twelve disciples to him and gave them authority to drive out evil spirits and to heal every disease and sickness"*. Then in *Mark 16:18* his final act before his ascension is to send them out into the whole world, to preach the good news accompanied by signs, including healings: *"...they will place their hands on sick people, and they will get well"*.

Examples of this gift in practice are found in *Acts chapter 3:1-10* where Peter heals the crippled beggar at the Beautiful Gate, and in *chapter 5, verses 15 and 16*, when *"Crowds gathered also from the towns around Jerusalem, bringing their sick and those tormented by evil spirits, and all of them were healed"*. The disciples were exercising the gifts of healing they had been given.

Church teaching on healing today

In the Anglican report **'The Church's Ministry of Healing'**, these words conclude the chapter on New Testament healings:

"To the Church, then, as the Body of Christ and as the Community through which the Holy Spirit works, command is given to heal the sick. Works of healing in the context of the Church's ministry throughout the ages are signs of the Kingdom of God to those who have eyes to see. Each act of healing is a direct, personal and creative act of God in fulfilment of his eternal purpose".

In 1999, the Catholic Church published a short document **'Instruction on Prayers for Healing'** which presented a very positive view of the gifts of healing and the healing ministry, together with some guidelines on liturgical services of healing.

It encouraged all of us to pray for healings, and reminded us that: **"Not only is it praiseworthy for individual members of the faithful to ask for healing for themselves and others, but the Church herself asks the Lord for the health of the sick in her liturgy".**

Everywhere people are looking for healing and wholeness, not just physical, spiritual, and emotional, but in society, and between nations and races. The following words from **Anglican Bishop Morris Maddocks** remind us that healing is all about Jesus. With the proliferation of New Age practices and other spiritualities, his advice is timely:

"Christian healing is, first and foremost, about Christ. It follows the pattern he set in his own ministry, and the commission he

gave to his own disciples; and the fact that it happens at all is the fruit of his work, both in the creation and salvation of mankind. In both these mighty works, humankind has been created and re-created in the image of God – has been made whole. It is the whole work of Christ in a person's body, mind, and spirit, designed to bring that person to that wholeness which is God's will for us."

We should all pray for the healing of sick people, and sometimes we will receive a supernatural gift of healing, meaning that the Lord will use us as his channels to bring healing to a person. Some people will be regularly used in this way, and it will be said that they exercise 'a ministry of healing', but healing will still only happen when God releases the gift.

6. Miraculous powers:

A miracle is a supernatural intervention in the ordinary course of nature; a temporary suspension or alteration of the natural order, brought about by the power of the Holy Spirit. In one sense all God's workings are miraculous, but what we are dealing with here is a specific supernatural act on the natural plane. Miraculous powers are a wonderful gift glorifying God, stimulating faith, and astonishing an unbelieving world.

The Scriptures are full of examples – the miracles performed by Moses in front of Pharaoh **Exodus chapters 7, 8, 9, 10, 11**; the parting of the red sea **Exodus 14:21**; Jesus turning water into wine **John 2:1-11**; the feeding of the 5,000 **John 6:5-15** and many more. In all these examples, the natural order is temporarily suspended, and the miraculous power of God takes over with amazing results.

Group Three – the 'speaking' or 'inspiration' gifts:

7. Prophecy:

One of the ways God speaks to us is very direct. He chooses certain people and uses them as his mouthpieces. They speak words directly to individuals, to communities, even to nations. The gift of prophecy is speaking a message from God inspired by the Holy Spirit. It does not add to the deposit of faith, but shows God is present and speaking to us. Every Christian shares in the prophetic office of Christ and is called to be a witness to the gospel message in word and deed, but what we are addressing here is different – it's a special grace given for a particular time and place.

In the simple gift of prophecy there is no revelation - just words of encouragement, edification, or comfort. As Paul explains in *1 Corinthians. 14:3 "Everyone who prophesies speaks to men for their strengthening, encouragement and comfort"*. This simple gift is available to everyone, which is why Paul writes in *1 Corinthians 14:1 "...eagerly desire the spiritual gifts, especially the gift of prophecy,"* and we should always be prepared for God to use us in this way.

But there is more to prophecy than just the simple gift of encouragement. The Old Testament prophets and John the Baptist (often described as the last of the Old Testament prophets) were specially chosen by God, and given a ministry of bringing his word to the people, often foretelling future events and warning of what was to come. There are several Old Testament accounts of the calling of prophets – *Isaiah chapter 6, Jeremiah chapter 1, Ezekiel chapters 2 and 3.* Here we find men who are specifically called by God and then sent to speak his word to the people. After John the Baptist, *"a man who was sent from God" John 1:6,* we still find men and women with a prophetic ministry who foretell future events, and this ministry of the prophet is listed in *Romans 12:6* and in *Ephesians 4:11* along with apostles, leaders, teachers, pastors, evangelists etc.

It is clear that these are all special callings which become a major part of a person's life, and so are not the same as a simple gift. When Jesus himself is rejected in Nazareth, he remarks *"...no prophet is accepted in his home town" Luke 4:24,* and in *Matthew 10:41* he teaches us that *"Anyone who receives a prophet because he is a prophet will receive a prophet's reward...".* Perhaps we are surprised to find in *1 Corinthians 12:28* that *"God has appointed first of all apostles, second prophets...."*. The ministry of a prophet is obviously seen by God as very important.

In *Acts 21:10-12* we have the example of Agabus giving Paul an acted-out prophecy:
"A prophet named Agabus came down from Judea. Coming over to us he took Paul's belt, tied his own hands and feet with it and said: The Holy Spirit says 'In this way the Jews of Jerusalem will bind the owner of this belt and will hand him over to the Gentiles'".
Agabus, inspired by the Spirit, came a long way to deliver this graphic prophetic word to prepare Paul for what would happen to him in Jerusalem. He also prophesies that a severe famine is coming, and the church in Antioch sends relief to the brethren in Judea, *Acts 11:27-30.* Others with this special ministry are *Judas*

called Barsabbas and Silas in Acts 15:32, and in Luke 2:36, the 84 year old widow Anna is described as a prophetess. The ministry of a prophet is clearly greatly valued in the early church, and the prophets "Judas (called Barsabbas) and Silas, two men who were leaders among the brothers" were sent to Antioch with Paul and Barnabas, as reported in Acts 15:22.

But there are many others who give prophetic words without being recognised as having specific callings to be prophets to the people, and there is evidence in the New Testament that this more simple gift of prophesying was common in the early Christian communities. In fact Paul's reason for writing about the spiritual gifts in his first letter to the Corinthians chapters 12, 13 and 14 is to correct some abuses that had crept into the church, with too many people prophetically giving public words of encouragement and speaking out in tongues.

One example of a number of people prophesying is found in Acts 19:6-7, when Paul baptises 12 men into the name of the Lord Jesus. As he lays his hands on them "the Holy Spirit came on them, and they spoke in tongues and prophesied". There is no suggestion here that they are called to be prophets, so we may assume they are giving simple prophetic words for "strengthening, encouragement and comfort" as Paul describes it in I Corinthians 14:3. In his discussion of prophecy in this chapter, Paul encourages the Corinthian Christians to "earnestly desire spiritual gifts, especially the gift of prophecy" verse 1, and in verse 5 "I would like every one of you to speak in tongues, but I would rather have you prophesy". This is clearly not about everyone having the special calling to be a prophet, but about bringing prophetic words of exhortation and encouragement to the assembled community.

So when it comes to prophecy, there is the simple gift and there is the special calling to a ministry – both are important and we must take them seriously. Recognised prophets will also often exercise the more simple gift of exhortation, encouragement and strengthening as shown in *Acts 15:32*, where *"Judas and Silas, who themselves were prophets, said much to encourage and strengthen the brothers"*.

"Weigh carefully what is said…" 1 Corinthians 14:29

But prophets will sometimes be wrong, so every prophetic word needs to be tested and this is primarily the responsibility of leadership, with the help of other prophets:

"Two or three prophets should speak, and the others should weigh carefully what is said" 1 Corinthians 14:29.

It is clear from Scripture that prophets come under the authority of the apostles. *"And in the church God has appointed first of all apostles, second prophets, third teachers…" 1 Cor. 12:28.* But it is also important to note that the church is *"built on the foundations of the apostles and prophets, with Christ Jesus himself as the chief cornerstone." Eph.2:20.* Prophets have a very important ministry in the church.

Only in Matthew's Gospel do we find this specific and rather dramatic warning of Jesus against the false prophets who will infiltrate his followers:

"Watch out for false prophets. They come to you in sheep's clothing, but inwardly they are ferocious wolves. By their fruit

you will recognise them" Matthew 7:15.

I think we can safely say that he was thinking of those who would come with distorted versions of the gospel, false claims to be the true messiah, or with a desire to cause disunity and lead people astray. But it is a timely warning of the need for testing and discernment, and an important part of this 'weighing' is the life and moral standing of the person who delivers the word – the prophet himself or herself.

With this goes the orthodoxy of the word itself and what it says about Jesus. *1 John 4:2-3* reminds us: *"This is how you can recognise the Spirit of God: every spirit that acknowledges that Jesus Christ has come in the flesh is from God, but every spirit that does not acknowledge Jesus is not from God".*

Paul echoes this in *1 Corinthians 12:3 "Therefore I tell you that no-one who is speaking by the Spirit of God says 'Jesus be cursed' and no-one can say 'Jesus is Lord' except by the Holy Spirit."*

In conclusion, it is important to remind ourselves that the style in which the prophetic word is delivered should not be a primary element in discerning its authenticity. In the Scriptures we can find examples of strange words, dreams, pictures, visions, actions, and unusual physical demonstrations. Any prophecy should, however, always be in line with Scripture and Church teaching, and be up-building even if it is challenging. A true word from God will always be life-giving. A question we might ask today - are there prophets in our church congregations and are they encouraged to speak out, or is this a gift we need to stir up again?

8. Different kinds of tongues:

Speaking in tongues is a supernatural utterance inspired by the Holy Spirit, in words the speaker has never learned and does not understand. It is a simple and basic gift, but the one people often find the most difficult to accept. It is probably the strangest of the spiritual gifts. Its primary use is in our private prayer life, so that we can praise and worship God freely without the limitation of using words we understand and feel are inadequate. In this usage it is the only spiritual gift not given for the benefit of others, although in a certain way the fact that my personal relationship with God is strengthened will be a benefit to the wider community. God gives us this gift so that we can speak to him from our hearts in total freedom. The mind can act as a dam when the rivers of living water pour out from our hearts, *John 7:37*, so when we need to overflow with praise God provides a temporary by-pass through the gift of speaking in tongues. In *1 Corinthians 14:2* Paul tells us *"For anyone who speaks in a tongue does not speak to men but to God"*.

Like every gift from God, speaking in tongues should be desired and actively sought, but it will not be given to everyone any more than the other gifts will. *1 Cor. 12:29-30 "Do all speak in tongues?"* implies that not everyone will speak in tongues, and this is consistent with our understanding of how gifts are given – to one this gift, to another that gift. Some classical Pentecostals regard speaking in tongues as the only acceptable evidence that someone has been baptised in the Holy Spirit, but this is not the view held by Catholics and most Protestants.

Paul seems to give almost contradictory teaching on this gift in

1 Corinthians 14. In *verse 5* he says: *"I would like every one of you to speak in tongues, but I would rather have you prophesy"*, and then *in verse 18 "I thank God that I speak in tongues more than all of you"*. It becomes clear if we read chapter 14 verses 1 to 25, that Paul is mainly dealing with speaking in tongues in public services, and is making the point that public messages in tongues do not edify others because unless they are interpreted, they are unintelligible. Prophetic words, however, bring encouragement that edifies the congregation. This is why I explained above that speaking in tongues is primarily for our private prayer times, as this is quite clearly the view of Paul. It seems there was disorder and confusion in the public meetings of the church at Corinth, with many people speaking out in tongues at the same time, and Paul is laying down some basic rules for good order.

As the gift of speaking in tongues is primarily for our private prayer, it will have a limited expression in public gatherings of the community. So public utterances in tongues should be few, and should always be interpreted so that everyone will understand the message. There is one exception or variation to this – singing in tongues.

Today we often experience singing in tongues, when people in a public gathering or service spontaneously begin to use the gift of tongues in song, in a most beautiful harmony and melody given by the Holy Spirit. It can only be described as praise and worship of God in a most inspiring way, and because it is addressed to God, no interpretation is to be expected. It is spontaneous, harmonious, and fades away as suddenly as it began.

Paul takes it as read that anyone can control the use of their gift of speaking in tongues - it is not an ecstatic utterance which takes us over, causing us to lose rational control of our actions. When the gift of speaking in tongues is used, it is never out of our control – we can stop speaking whenever we wish.

As **Rev. Larry Christenson**, a Lutheran priest, explains it: **"The idea that a speaker in tongues goes off into a kind of religious ecstasy, where he loses both emotional and personal control, is contrary both to Scripture and actual experience. The person who exercises this gift is perfectly able to remain in full control of himself and his emotions."**

In addition to *1 Corinthians chapters 12 and 14*, examples of the gift of different kinds of tongues are to be found in *Acts 10:46* when the Holy Spirit came upon the household of Cornelius, *"For they heard them speaking in tongues and praising God"*, and in *Acts 19:6 in Ephesus "When Paul placed his hands on them, the Holy Spirit came on them, and they spoke in tongues and prophesied."* The gift of tongues is certainly a sign of the presence of the Holy Spirit, and this is one reason Paul encourages us to seek it.

But our understanding of the normal use of the gift of tongues should be based on the practical teaching of Paul in *1 Corinthians chapters 12 to 14*, as we know that Paul spoke in tongues himself and has first-hand experience of the value and use of the gift. It is also clear from Paul's teaching that in its normal use it is unintelligible both to the speaker and to the hearers, which forms the basis for his clear assertion that when used publicly it is inferior to the gift of prophecy, which everyone can understand. In *1 Corinthians 14: 12-13* he explains his thinking: *"Since you are eager to have spiritual gifts, try to excel in gifts that build up the church. For this reason anyone who speaks in a tongue should pray that he may interpret what he says"*. This also strengthens his view that tongues are primarily a gift for private prayer: *"For anyone who speaks in a tongue does not speak to men but to God. Indeed no one understands him; he utters mysteries with his spirit" 14: 2.*

People are sometimes confused about the gift of tongues when they read how it was given to the disciples in a particular way at Pentecost: *"When they heard this sound, a crowd came together in bewilderment, because each one heard them speaking in his own language" Acts 2:6.* Experience shows that a tongue in the language of a listener is quite rare today, although this was clearly the experience of the crowds on Pentecost Day. But in *1 Corinthians chapters 12 to 14* we have Paul's reliable teaching on the ways the gift of tongues is normally used – in our private prayer, and occasionally in a public meeting with an interpretation. The Pentecost Day experience of the gift clearly demonstrated the presence of the Holy Spirit and caught the crowd's attention, as many languages not known to the disciples were spoken. Our experience today is that just occasionally a public message given in tongues may be in a language someone present knows, but usually such a message will require interpretation.

In concluding the section on this unusual gift, I offer **St. Teresa of Avila's** experience, as described in her book **'The Interior Castle'**: **"Our Lord sometimes gives the soul feelings of jubilation and a strange prayer it doesn't understand. I am writing about this favour here so that if he grants it to you, you may give him such praise and know what is taking place. It seems like gibberish,** and certainly the experience is like that, for it is a joy so excessive that the soul wouldn't want to enjoy it alone, but wants to tell everyone about it so that they might help this soul to praise our Lord. Oh what blessedness, sisters! If only God would give it to us all!"

Similarly, writing On the *Psalms 99.3 and 97.4*, St. Augustine describes it like this:
"One who jubilates does not utter words but a certain sound of joy without words; for it is the voice of the soul poured forth in joy, expressing as far as possible what it feels without reflecting on the meaning". "If you cannot express your joy, jubilate; jubilation expresses your joy if you cannot speak. Let not your joy be silent".

St. Gregory the Great in Moralia 8.89 puts it this way:
"...we call it jubilus when we conceive such joy in the heart as we cannot give vent to by the force of words, and yet the triumph of the heart vents with the voice what it cannot give forth by speech. Now the mouth is rightly said to be filled with laughter, the lips with jubilation, since in that eternal land when the mind of the righteous is borne away in transport, the tongue is lifted up in the song of praise".

This sounds very like what Paul writes about in *Ephesians 5:19: "Speak to one another with psalms, hymns and spiritual songs. Sing and make music in your heart to the Lord, always giving thanks to God the Father for everything..."*

9. The interpretation of tongues:
This is the supernatural interpretation, into a language known to

the hearers, of the meaning of a message delivered in tongues. It is an interpretation, not a direct translation. The purpose is clearly to render the gift of tongues intelligible so that the hearers may all be edified. Interpretation is important when the message is given in tongues at a public meeting – it is not required for our private prayer in tongues. When someone begins to speak publicly in tongues, a person will be given the gift of interpretation, and will immediately be open to the guidance of the Holy Spirit so that they are available to bring the interpretation when inspired to do so. The interpretation is sometimes given by the same person who spoke out in tongues – *"anyone who speaks in a tongue should pray that he may interpret what he says" I Cor. 14:13.*

As we have already seen, the New Testament teaching on the interpretation of tongues is to be found in *1 Corinthians 14*, where Paul gives examples of good and bad practice. When a message in tongues is given in a public meeting or service and then interpreted by someone in the congregation, the effect is to powerfully focus the attention of all who are present on what God is saying.

Stirrings of the Holy Spirit

So having looked at the charisms, also known as special spiritual graces, listed in *1 Corinthians 12*, we need to remember that in this context our use of the word 'spiritual' has a particular meaning which relates it directly to the Holy Spirit. We do not just mean supernatural, because as we know from *Ephesians chapter 6*, there are many other supernatural powers and spirits in the heavenly realms.

A message of knowledge or wisdom, a prophetic word, a gift of faith or healing, these can change a person's life in a moment, in a way that years of therapy or treatment may never achieve. When someone is instantly healed of an obvious sickness, when the blind see, the lame walk, we are immediately aware that God is at work among us. We need God's help to challenge the things that are wrong in our society, and to bring wholeness and freedom to people who are suffering. This is why we must always be open to the work of the Spirit and willing to be used as channels for his gifts.

Perhaps **St. Hilary of Poitiers** can have the last word:
"We who have been reborn through the sacrament of baptism experience intense joy when we feel within us the first stirrings of the Holy Spirit. We begin to have insight into the mysteries of faith; we are able to prophesy and speak with wisdom. We become steadfast in hope and receive abundant gifts of healing. Demons are made subject to our authority. These gifts enter us like a gentle rain, and... little by little, they bear abundant fruit"
(Tract on the Psalms, 64.14-15.)

None of these gifts are delegated to us by higher church authorities. We receive them because we are baptised and open to the Holy Spirit. Entry into the spiritual gifts comes when we are willing to let the Holy Spirit use us. It's as simple as that - we just need the courage to pray:

Come, Holy Spirit!

Discuss these statements with reference to the Scriptures:

These special gifts or charisms are supernatural, given by the Spirit as he chooses, and may be given to anyone who has received the Holy Spirit

The charisms in this study are those listed in chapter 12 of St. Paul's first letter to the Corinthian Christians, and are the ones about which there is a lot of ignorance.

The Scriptures:

1 Corinthians 12, Romans 12:6-8, Ephesians 4: 11-12

The Questions:

Am I familiar with the gifts of the Holy Spirit, and have I ever exercised any of these charisms?

CHAPTER FIVE

THE GIFTS OF THE HOLY SPIRIT

- **Why do we need the spiritual gifts?**
- **What do we mean by 'spiritual'?**
- **How are we to use these gifts of the Spirit?**

WHY DO WE NEED THE SPIRITUAL GIFTS?

We need the gifts of the Holy Spirit just as much today as in the early church, but sadly few people even know they are available. All these gifts and ministries of the Holy Spirit, as well as others we have not considered, contribute to the basic message of loving, caring, sharing, and serving, to which every Christian is called. Today we may be much more sophisticated than the early Christians and know more about many things, but there are still physical, mental, and emotional needs which can only be met in the power of the Spirit. What is needed is the realisation that all the spiritual gifts are still available today to those who open their lives to the presence and power of the Holy Spirit. The spiritual gifts we have been considering are given to build up our faith, to bring wholeness to different areas of our lives, to show that we are a community dependent on one another, and to bring glory to God through the extension of his Kingdom. We need to understand the gifts and recognise their importance, praying that the Holy Spirit will pour them out among us.

WHAT DO WE MEAN BY 'SPIRITUAL'?

By 'spiritual' we mean:
- **of the Holy Spirit**
- **in the Holy Spirit**
- **formed by the Holy Spirit**
- **by the power of the Holy Spirit**
- **with the character of the Holy Spirit**
- **showing the fruit of the Holy Spirit**

We are studying gifts that come to us from God to help us build up the Christian community, meet individual needs, and become more effective witnesses to the message of the Gospel and the person of Jesus Christ.

Paul reminds us in *1 Corinthians 12:4-6:*
"There are different kinds of gifts, but the same Spirit. There are different kinds of service, but the same Lord. There are different kinds of working, but the same God works all of them in all men".

And in verse 12:
"The body is a unit, though it is made up of many parts; and though all its parts are many, they form one body."

And in verse 14:
"Now the body is not made up of one part but of many."

And in verse 27:
"Now you are the body of Christ, and each one of you is a part of it".

These Scriptures remind us that though we are all different, we are in this together. We need each other, we are inter-dependent, so my gift is for you and yours is for me. We may pray for specific gifts for ourselves, but need to accept that the very nature of any gift is that it is not earned or merited, but is freely given as the Giver decides, not as the recipient demands. Above all, it is the Giver we seek, not just his gifts.

They are God's gifts, not ours

It is wonderful to receive these amazing gifts, and to be used by God to bring his wholeness to others, but we must use them only as he requires, and always under the guidance of the Holy Spirit. We do not possess them, they are his, we are merely the channels he chooses to bring his life-changing power to others. The answer to our next question will help us see how this works when it comes to exercising the gifts of the Holy Spirit.

SO HOW ARE WE TO USE THESE GIFTS OF THE HOLY SPIRIT?

We have seen that the gifts of the Holy Spirit are not given to us for our private benefit, but for the good of all of us. They are available to anyone who has decided to give the Spirit freedom to work in and through him or her. Paul emphasises that these special gifts are given to build up the faith and spiritual power of the church community, so that others will be drawn to share in the joy and abundant life they see before them. They are, therefore, tools to build up the body, rather than an end to be sought in themselves. We have considered the list of individual gifts given by Paul in **1 Corinthians chapter 12**, and have briefly looked at some of his instructions on how they are to be used, which we find in *chapter 14*. It is hardly a coincidence that between these two chapters we find in *chapter 13* Paul's great teaching on love.

Gifts plus Love

Taken in its context, **1 Corinthians 13** is really about gifts plus love, and is an illustration rather than an exhortation. The exhortation follows in the first sentence of *chapter 14: "Follow the way of love and eagerly desire spiritual gifts..."*

In *chapter 13* Paul is telling us to be practical about love – it's not just some vague feeling or emotional response, it's about how we behave at home, at work, in the shops, in our places of leisure, in our church. The good way is to know all about the gifts God wants us to have - the excellent way is to use those gifts in an atmosphere of love: *"I will show you the most excellent way"* **12: 31**.

God is love, **1 John 4:8,16,** and the gifts of the Spirit come from God. In themselves they are good gifts from a loving God, but the manifestation of them will reveal the love or lack of love in a church, group, or community. Today we may think we have love, but often that's not really true. We meet each other on a rather superficial and polite level, and it's easy to maintain a good relationship at arm's length. But let us get close, involved, mixed up in each other's day-to-day lives, and we'll soon discover how strong our love really is. As Jesus reminds us in **John 13:35: "By this all men will know that you are my disciples, if you love one another",** and the writer to the Hebrews exhorts us to *"Keep*

on loving each other" Hebrews 13:1.
Exercising any charism is an act of love:

In 1 Corinthians chapter 13 Paul tells us that:
- love is patient
- love bears all things
- love always believes the best
- love endures
- love keeps on loving
- love holds on even when I let people down again and again
- love always hopes for the best

So how do we stand up to the test of this love that is so essential, the heart of the message of Christianity, a reflection of the very nature of God? It's not just a matter of how we feel – it involves our will. It's an agape love that deliberately chooses its object, and goes on loving through thick and thin. It will dominate not just our emotions and intellect, but also our will. Christianity is the only religion that says *"God is love" 1 John 4:8,16* and when you and I love, we become more like God. The gifts of the Holy Spirit are given to us by a loving God and are to be used in a climate of love. Just as a human body needs lubricating fluid to help it to function, so love is what makes the church, the body of Christ, function properly.

Our claims to be full of the Holy Spirit are meaningless if our attitudes and our behaviour do not show love. It's the first fruit that grows in us, showing that the Holy Spirit is present and at work. Gifts and ministries are dangerous and ineffective without love. What do I mean by this?

Building up the body

The gifts of the Spirit are given to build up the body of Christ, and this includes our local church. When Paul wrote **1 Corinthians**, he was sending a pastoral letter to a local church, with instructions on how to do things properly. Now we all know what it means to be part of a local church – the joys and sorrows, the encouragements and frustrations, the cliques and factions, the progressives and the conservatives, the passionate and the luke-warm, the friendly and the aloof – all presided over by the priest or pastor who is trying to listen to the Lord, preach his word, celebrate the sacraments, give some direction, and keep everything going. In this complex mix we should find the gifts of the Holy Spirit being used. The fact that this may not normally be our experience simply means that we are not living in the fullness of what God intends for us, and we may not have the right priorities. Where there is genuine love, relationships are good and a parish is moving forward, the gifts will be given and received with thanksgiving and will bear fruit. Where there is little love and no real vision, we will find jealousy, disagreement, and division – ground in which the fruit cannot grow, and in which we are not likely to find the gifts of the Holy Spirit being freely used.

This is why Paul teaches us that love is so important:
- **love is harmony, not division**
- **love is humility, not arrogance**
- **love builds, it does not destroy**
- **love is sensitive, not over-bearing**
- **love means being willing to restrict my liberty for the sake of another**

The gifts of the Spirit will test our love for one another. When I know you love me, I will accept almost anything from you – so the Lord can use you to minister to me. If I'm not sure that you love me, I will be hesitant about receiving anything from you.

God often gives spiritual gifts to young, immature Christians - he knows they'll usually have the courage to step out in faith and use the gifts. But this often provokes jealousy – "why has God given her that gift when I've been faithful all these years and she's only been here five minutes?" We need to remember that the gifts speak about the Giver and the beneficiary, not about the channel, and they are given to build up the church community. The exercise of the gifts of the Spirit does not depend on a person being mature, holy, or even in a state of grace. But if the gifts are to be fully effective, they must always be used in love.

So the most important part of the answer to our question "how are we to use these gifts of the Holy Spirit?" is – use them in love.

And in good order

Paul then goes on in *chapter 14* to tell us that they must also be used in an orderly way: *"When you come together, everyone has a hymn, or a word of instruction, a revelation, a tongue or an interpretation. All of these must be done for the strengthening of the church" verse 26.*

In the early church it seems that people came together bursting to give. They were so stirred up by the Holy Spirit that they needed rules to maintain order and stop the meeting getting out of control – hardly our problem today!

What Paul is teaching the *Corinthians* in *chapter 14* is that there must always be:
- **sensitivity to those around us**
- **sensitivity to the glory of God**
- **a limiting of the gifts sometimes, to maintain good order**
- **testing of the gifts by others**
- **respect for authority and church structure**
- **co-operation with the Holy Spirit**
- **co-operation within the body**
- **submission to the Lordship of Jesus**
- **submission to the authority of Scripture**
- **submission to the teaching authority of the Church**

"For God is not a God of disorder but of peace" verse 33, and "….everything should be done in a fitting and orderly way" verse 40.

This means that I must restrain my gift if it cannot be made edifying to the church assembly, and I must restrain my participation according to the teaching on the functions and relationships between members of the church. I must only use my gift in accordance with the teaching of Scripture, and under the authority of the local leadership. It is one thing to receive an inspiration from the Holy Spirit – it is quite another thing to know when and how to use it. This is something the Lord will teach us, often through our leaders and mentors.

To use the spiritual gifts properly and effectively we need:
1. **Faith**
2. **Love**
3. **Time**

4.   Good order
Tools for a job

God wants us to have the gifts of his Holy Spirit, so we must desire them and ask for them. He will not force them upon us, but without them we are impoverished, and much more limited in our ability to meet the needs of those around us. The gifts are not going to come because we sit around and lament their absence – we need to teach about them and encourage people to ask for them in expectant faith. When we are used by God as channels to help others, our faith increases, we become more committed, and as a result can be used by God to even greater effect. The gifts of the Holy Spirit are not some exotic super-spiritual novelties, they are for here and now where we live and act – where we laugh, cry, love, work, and suffer. The gifts are tools for a job, and the job is to produce better fruit. We don't need a spade at the top of a tree – we need it down at the bottom in the mud. Gifts are not a sign of spiritual maturity, but fruit is, and we will move on to look at the fruit in the next chapter.

It is my hope that, at the end of this chapter, we'll have a better understanding of the spiritual gifts, that we'll have realised why we need them, and how we are to use them. Perhaps some of the ignorance to which Paul referred will have been dispelled. But the question is still there - do we want these gifts? If so, are we prepared to ask the Holy Spirit for them, and then to step out in faith and use them as he stirs them up within us, knowing that not everyone will agree with what we're doing? It takes courage to stand up for what we believe when we know we'll be challenged. If we're willing to step outside our comfort zones and follow God in faith, we will be tested. Every time we're prepared to stand for something, or to try something new, there will always be someone to tell us we're wrong. We need the courage of our convictions.

In the early Church, the Pentecost experience of the presence and power of the Holy Spirit was very much alive, and candidates for baptism expected to receive charismatic gifts. This is clearly expressed by **St. Cyril of Jerusalem: "My final words, beloved ones, in this instruction are words of exhortation, urging all of you to prepare your souls for the reception of the heavenly charisms" (Catechetical Lectures).**

In May 1998, at the meeting of the ecclesial movements and new communities, **Pope John Paul II** exhorted us: **"Open yourselves docilely to the gifts of the Spirit! Accept gratefully and obediently the charisms which the Spirit never ceases to bestow on us!"**

If we take the risk, ask for the gifts of the Holy Spirit, and then use them as the Spirit directs us, we'll reach heights we thought were beyond us, and we'll see God at work changing people's lives by his love and power, and building up his church.

Come, Holy Spirit!

*Discuss these statements
with reference to the Scriptures:*

Charisms are given to enrich the lives of all of us,
to build up the church, and to enable us to spread
the Kingdom of God more effectively

The Gifts of the Spirit are given
so that we can serve others

Each gift is for a particular purpose,
and will be used in a certain way

The Scriptures:

1 Corinthians Chapters 13 and 14

The Questions:

How do the charisms help us to evangelise?

How are we to use the gifts of the Holy
Spirit in our group and in our church?

CHAPTER SIX

THE FRUIT OF THE HOLY SPIRIT

- **What is the fruit of the Holy Spirit?**
- **The fruit of the Spirit is the nature of Jesus becoming more and more visible in our lives. What does this mean?**
- **How is the fruit produced in our lives?**
- **Why are we expected to bear fruit?**

When we think of fruit, what comes to mind is something that appeals to our senses. We may see images of plants, bushes, and trees, all bearing different kinds, colours, shapes, and textures of fruit. We'll all have our favourites - fruit is something attractive, delicious, enjoyable. We don't make fruit in a factory – it grows, and good fruit is a clear sign of a good, healthy bush or tree.

WHAT IS THE FRUIT OF THE HOLY SPIRIT?

In *Galatians 5:22-23* Paul describes the fruit of the Spirit in these words:

"But the fruit of the Spirit is love, joy, peace, patience, kindness, goodness, faithfulness, gentleness and self-control. Against such things there is no law".

To express it in a very simple way, the fruit listed here is a display of the character of God himself, as revealed to us in the person of Jesus his Son during his time on earth. It's what should result from the new life of Christ, born in us at our baptism, and present through the in-dwelling Holy Spirit. When this kind of fruit is evident in our lives, it shows that through God's grace, the sanctifying power of the Holy Spirit is working in us – that we are good 'trees' bearing ripe fruit. Jesus reminds us: *"A good tree cannot bear bad fruit, and a bad tree cannot bear good fruit" Matthew 7:18.*

The fruits are the good and attractive qualities that God produces in us, reflecting his goodness to us. They originate in his action within us that produces new life, creates a new relationship with him, with ourselves, and with our neighbour.

Such a new relationship has no pretence or superficiality because it comes from something real – true love, joy, peace, patience, kindness, goodness, faithfulness, gentleness and self-control. When these qualities can be seen, then clearly the Holy Spirit is at work, and others will recognise the presence and power of God in us. *"By their fruit you will recognise them"*, as Jesus tells us in *Matthew 7:16.*

The gifts of the Spirit and the fruit of the Spirit are quite distinct and different:

- **The gifts of the Holy Spirit enable us to do what Jesus did**
  - **• • • The fruit of the Spirit enables us to be like Jesus was**
- **The gifts are many**

••• The fruit is one – the divine nature
• The gifts are expressed corporately
••• The fruit is shown individually.

Fruit is the clearest outward sign of the Holy Spirit's presence; the gifts are tools to help us to produce fruit.

THE FRUIT OF THE SPIRIT IS THE NATURE OF JESUS BECOMING MORE EVIDENT IN OUR LIVES. WHAT EXACTLY DO WE MEAN BY THIS?

One fruit with nine flavours

The list of the fruit of the Spirit consists of everything we would like to be:

loving, joyful, peaceful, patient, kind, good, faithful, gentle and self-controlled.

I think it helps if we think of it as the nature of Jesus – one fruit with nine distinct flavours. If people see these qualities in us, they are seeing the character and personality of Jesus Christ, so let's take a brief look at each flavour:

Love comes first, because without it the other eight flavours would not exist. It's the new command of Jesus *"Love one another" John 13:34,* and *"...the most excellent way" 1 Corinthians 12:31.* It is entirely giving *"For God so loved the world that he gave* *his one and only Son..." John 3:16.*

Joy is exciting and liberating. Knowing Christ fills us with "...*an inexpressible and glorious joy..." 1 Peter 1:8* which others should see, *"for the joy of the Lord is your strength" Nehemiah 8:10.*

Peace is calmness, security, harmony, wholeness, completeness, assurance – God's supernatural rest in the midst of confusion and difficulties. Whilst it is a flavour of the fruit of the Spirit *Galatians 5:22* it is also a gift of Christ *"Peace I leave with you, my peace I give you" John 14:27.*

Patience is self-restraint, tolerance, endurance, long-temperedness – *"The Lord is gracious and compassionate, slow to anger and rich in love" Psalm 145:8.* Our patience is based on the indisputable fact that God is at work in our lives.

Kindness is compassion, sympathy, mellowness – a quality that comes from the heart *"Be kind and compassionate to one another..." Ephesians 4:32.*

Goodness is unstinted generosity, a way to express love in action, being generous with ourselves and what we have. Just as God is good and so are his actions, *"You are good and what you do is good" Psalm 119:68,* so our goodness should be seen in our actions.

Faithfulness is complete trust, unquestioning belief, reliability, confidence – it's what the Christian life is all about. God has shown himself to be faithful, to keep his promises, so we know we can put our faith in him. God is looking for faithfulness, not necessarily for success as we would see it. *"Well done, good and faithful servant! You have been faithful with a few things; I will put you in charge of many things" Matthew 25:21.*

Gentleness is humility, lack of pride, meekness, not being resentful. Jesus explains it like this: *"Take my yoke upon you and learn from me, for I am gentle and humble in heart, and you will find rest for your souls" Matthew 11:29.* Or as St Paul puts it *"Brothers, if someone is caught in a sin, you who are spiritual should restore him gently" Gal. 6:1.*

Self-Control is the last in the list. It is self-restraint, moderation, temperance – it binds together all the other flavours of the fruit of the Spirit, and shows that God is at work in our lives. In today's consumerist and individualistic world, self-control is less and less valued, but Paul tells us: *"For the grace of God... teaches us to say 'No' to ungodliness and worldly passions, and to live self-controlled, upright and godly lives in this present age..." Titus 2:11-12.*

Freedom and Law

At the end of this list of the fruit of the Spirit, Paul says to the Galatian Christians *"Against such things there is no law" Gal. 5:23.* St. Augustine said something similar in another way: **"Love God, and do as you please"** – the first two words giving restraint to the rest. When the fruit of the Spirit is evident in our lives, it means that our desires have been re-focused and we want to be like Jesus. If this is so, laws are not needed because we will want to please Jesus and do what he asks of us. Love will be our law. Laws are designed to stop people hurting each other, but where love is in control, laws are not necessary. Living freely under the guidance of love is God's way of life for us, but it is foreign to our natural understanding and desires. Where there is a willingness to live in joyful obedience to Jesus, no law would be needed, but sadly in our western society, more and more laws seem to be needed as we move further and further away from God's law of love.

Are we foolish too?

Earlier in his letter to the Galatians, Paul had challenged them:

"Are you so foolish? After beginning with the Spirit, are you now trying to attain your goal by human effort? Does God give you his Spirit and work miracles among you because you observe the law, or because you believe what you heard?" Galatians 3:3,5.

There is this battle within us between freedom and law. We easily give up our freedom for the security of knowing what is expected of us, what is going to happen next, and how we are to act - but this allows the Holy Spirit very little room in which to work. The traditions and rules by which we live bring us security; the idea that we could let go of some of these and allow the Spirit to guide us is too frightening to contemplate. But the only way the fruit will grow is if we allow the Holy Spirit freedom to work in us.

There must be a passion for freedom in our hearts – we must be determined to follow the voice of the Holy Spirit even when it means breaking established habits. There is a narrow way between liberty in love and security of habit, and the temptation to give up the struggle is always strong. We must resist it.

SO HOW IS THE FRUIT
PRODUCED IN OUR LIVES?

We need to provide the right conditions if the life of Christ is to flourish and the fruit grow in us. Ripe fruit hanging from the branches of a tree clearly shows that it's a good tree and has been well cared for.

When people hear someone talking about being open to the Holy Spirit and see obvious changes in that person's life, they'll listen - they can see the fruit. But if a tree is to produce good fruit it must be cultivated, pruned, nurtured, and protected against disease and attacks by pests, so that the fruit can ripen and be harvested at the right time. We too will produce better fruit if we allow ourselves to be cultivated, pruned, nurtured, and protected. This is where the gifts of the Spirit play an important part – they are tools to produce better fruit in the lives of all of us by addressing those areas where we need to change and to grow. A fruit tree also needs the right conditions – water, sunshine, fertiliser, good soil. We need these things too:

- **the water of the Spirit**
- **the sunshine of God's love**
- **the fertiliser of prayer**
- **the good soil of the Word of God and the Sacraments.**

Can others see the fruit?

God is interested in every Christian who starts life as a seedling, is fed and protected, blossoms in the fullness of time, and is expected to bear good fruit.

The primary purpose of every plant, bush, or tree is to bear fruit - this is the way it reproduces itself. People looking at Christians should be able to see the fruit, and recognise the work of God in us. The fruit of the Spirit will attract them, and cause them to want to be like us. But good fruit takes time to grow and we must be patient.

The Seed

In fruit-bearing plants, the life of the plant is in the seed. The farmer does not create the life, it's already present in the seed, but he must ensure the best conditions for that seed to germinate and grow into a new plant. The field will need to be prepared - weeded, dug over, and fertilised. Our lives may be like a field overgrown with weeds, and used as a dumping ground for all sorts of rubbish. We need to acknowledge this, and decide to clear it up. There will be some things we can do ourselves, but above all we need to ask Jesus to work with us through his Holy Spirit. When he gets access to the field – by our invitation – he can start to push things around, to clear away the rubbish that clutters up our lives, to help us re-order our priorities, to work with us to pull out the weeds of sin, and to break up the ground of our hard-heartedness. But he won't do anything without us – he needs our co-operation. The fruit is a result of the work of the Spirit within us, and we will need to acknowledge that there are problems in some areas of our lives and hand them over to God. Then we must be obedient as he starts working with us.

Pruning

Every gardener knows that in order to produce good fruit, a bush or tree must be pruned – excess and unnecessary growth has to be

removed. Jesus tells us in *John chapter 15: 1-4:*
"I am the true vine, and my Father is the gardener. He cuts off every branch in me that bears no fruit, while every branch that does bear fruit he prunes so that it will be even more fruitful. You are already clean because of the word I have spoken to you. Remain in me, and I will remain in you. No branch can bear fruit by itself; it must remain in the vine. Neither can you bear fruit unless you remain in me".

The message is clear. We are to remain in Christ, and to accept that some things will have to be pruned – relationships, activities, even ministries and services – so that our lives can be more fruitful.

Fruit grows
Fruit grows – it is not made by us. We do not provide the dynamic, vital force by which God's fruit grows any more than we provide the original seed. It is all of God, but it does require our co-operation. Because the Spirit is alive within us, we will bear fruit, but it will only grow as we surrender more and more to the Divine Gardener. It's his garden, and the fruit is for him. When we desire to live a fuller life in the Holy Spirit, we want the fruit in our lives to increase, and this will happen as long as we are open and do not put up barriers. Much of our slow growth in the things of God is due to the fact that we have some clearing up and sorting out to do, and we are not prepared to receive nearly as much help as we need and he wants to give us. Sometimes our desires are conditional rather than absolute, and this restricts what the Holy Spirit is able to do in us. If there is little sign of the Holy Spirit's fruit in our lives, it may sometimes be that we are in a dormant period when God is strengthening our roots, but it is often because we are not co-operating as we should.

Paul tells us in *Romans 11:16 that "...if the root is holy, so are the branches", and in Colossians 2: 6-7 "...just as you received Christ Jesus as Lord, continue to live in him, rooted and built up in him, strengthened in the faith you were taught, and overflowing with thankfulness."* We need to be well rooted in Christ if we're going to bear good fruit.

If the fruit of the Spirit is growing in us and is clearly visible to others, this will help us to fulfil the words of Jesus in *John 15:8-11* when he speaks about another kind of fruit. Here he is talking about our fruitfulness in bringing others into relationship with him. In this context, our fruitfulness is to be seen when our witness to our faith produces new disciples of Jesus.

- That God may be glorified: *"This is to my Father's glory, that you bear much fruit" Jn.15:8*
- That we may show we are disciples of Jesus his Son: *"...showing yourselves to be my disciples" Jn 15:8*
- That the joy of the Lord may be in us: *"...so that my joy may be in you and that your joy may be complete." Jn.15:11.*

The testimony we give, the position we hold in our church, the denomination to which we belong – these say nothing about our spiritual life. The only real evidence we have is the fruit that the Holy Spirit causes to grow in us. The one desire common to every form of life is to reproduce itself, to be fruitful. This is true for Christians – each person who has come into new life in Christ is called to reproduce this divine life. The fruit of the Spirit is Christ's personality expressed through us. When we allow this to grow in every part of our lives, it is Jesus, the first fruit, who will be evident.

It has nothing to do with self-effort; it's not Christian character manufactured by some kind of human ability. It's not according to me, it's according to Him. When we look at the fruit of the Spirit, we are looking at something we want Him to achieve in us with our co-operation.

We must allow the Holy Spirit to form the life of Jesus in us, so that the world can see Him in us and through us. This will happen as the fruit of the Spirit grows in us.

Come, Holy Spirit!

*Discuss these statements
with reference to the Scriptures:*

**The Fruit of the Holy Spirit is the nature of Jesus
becoming more and more evident in our lives**

It is really one Fruit with nine flavours

**The Fruit of the Spirit grows in us, we cannot produce it
ourselves, but we need to provide the right conditions
by asking Jesus to help us deal with the obstacles and
hindrances that interfere with its growth**

The Scriptures:

Galatians 5: 13-26 and John chapter 15

The Questions:

Why do we need to bear fruit?

**Which of the flavours of the fruit of the
Spirit is struggling to grow in my life?**

CHAPTER SEVEN

THE NEW LIFE -
WALKING IN THE SPIRIT

- **What do we mean by walking in the Spirit, and how do we do it?**
- **What are the dangers we must guard against?**
- **How do we stay with the Spirit, and not slip back into the old ways?**

WHAT DO WE MEAN BY 'WALKING IN THE SPIRIT' AND HOW DO WE DO IT?

In the earlier chapters we have seen that the Holy Spirit is a person, promised by the Father, and released to us after Jesus had ascended. He is the presence, the love, the power, and the life of God, given to us here and now to renew us in our relationship to God, to ourselves, and to others. The Spirit is available in his fullness to every Christian, and when he is poured out to work in us he reveals Jesus as Lord and Saviour, God as a loving Father, and brings love, power, authority, and commitment into our lives. This means that every area of our lives can be renewed and revitalised.

In chapter 36, verses 26 and 27, the prophet *Ezekiel* prophesied God's plan:

"I will give you a new heart and put a new spirit in you; I will remove from you your heart of stone and give you a heart of flesh. And I will put my Spirit in you and move you to follow my decrees and be careful to keep my laws".

And Zechariah, in chapter 4 verse 6, reminded us of God's requirements: *"Not by might, nor by power, but by my Spirit, says the Lord Almighty."*

New Life in the Spirit

So, inspired by the Old Testament prophets, when we talk about walking in the Spirit we mean living this new life, with this new heart, in the love and strength of the Holy Spirit and not by our own might or power.

At its most simple, walking in the Spirit means walking with God, in complete unity with him and his purposes, directed and guided by his Holy Spirit. It means putting into practice day after day the new life that Jesus has made available to us. *"Since we live by the Spirit, let us keep in step with the Spirit" Galatians 5:25.*

Jesus explained it to Nicodemus like this:

"I tell you the truth, no one can enter the kingdom of God unless he is born of water and the Spirit. Flesh gives birth to flesh, but the Spirit gives birth to spirit. You should not be surprised at my saying 'you must be born again'. The wind blows wherever it pleases. You hear its sound, but you cannot tell where it comes from or where it is going. So it is with everyone born of the Spirit" John 3:5-8.

We are born again when we enter this new life through Baptism and the coming of the Holy Spirit, but living it out is not automatic. Even though we know all about it, and want to walk in the Spirit and enjoy this new life, the old life is still open to us and we must be aware of this.

What is the old life?

It's a life lived largely by rules. We see Jesus Christ as a man who lived 2,000 years ago, we believe that he is God, sent to us by his Father, and we try to follow his teaching and to do as he did. We take on his ideals and try to live by them. So we see Christianity as a way of life governed by a set of rules, and we try by using our willpower to do what is right, and to live as we believe Jesus would want us to live. This approach is very similar to that of the Jewish people at the time of Christ – they tried to live by the law but failed. Even those who wanted to live by the law could not do so, and those whose task it was to teach the law also failed to put it into practice in their own lives or to help others, and came in for harsh condemnation from Jesus:

"And you experts in the law, woe to you, because you load people down with burdens they can hardly carry, and you yourselves will not lift one finger to help them" **Luke 11:46.**

When we look at the teachings of Jesus, at the **Sermon on the Mount** for example, we realise that with only the law to help us we will find it impossible to put them into practice in our lives. Neither a new law nor a new idealism are enough on their own – we need new life.

So what is the new life?

It is life in the Holy Spirit, God at work in us. Jesus has supplied us with the power to live a new life through his Holy Spirit – we provide the channel. This means that we rely more on God working in us and through us, than on our own efforts to be good and to do the right things. It is a completely new principle of life, not just a few adjustments made to the old way of life.

How do we enter into this new life?

We've already seen in chapters 2 and 3 that when we are thirsty, Jesus invites us to come to him and drink *John 7:37.* He is the source of the new life.

If we acknowledge our need and want to have new life in the Spirit, then with expectant faith we must ask him to baptise us in his Holy Spirit. God has promised and he will honour his promise; any barriers to receiving from him will lie with us and not with him. We have already looked at what we mean when we speak of being baptised in the Spirit in chapter 3 – an unconditional surrender to the work of the Spirit in us.

How do we then live this new life in the Holy Spirit?

Sometimes life in the Spirit is thought to be anything that is supernatural – that simply because something is supernatural means it must be in accordance with the Holy Spirit. But we have seen that the Holy Spirit is not the only source of supernatural power, so we need to be careful. If we always equate the supernatural with the Holy Spirit, then it is an easy but dangerous step to define life in the Spirit as life surrounded by supernatural events. Of course some of what the Holy Spirit does is clearly supernatural – the manifestation of his gifts, for example. But the key to living and walking in the Spirit is being led by the Holy Spirit in both natural and supernatural ways.

To walk in the Spirit is not just to receive direct guidance from God in everything. We are also led by the Spirit when we allow God to form us in other ways – through studying the Scriptures, teaching, prayer, our commitment to the sacraments and to the life of the Church, and through the Christian community. No one should wait for a direct indication from the Holy Spirit before doing something they know to be right and necessary. Our approach to many things has already been formed by the Lord, and we can remain open to the Spirit without seeking direct guidance for every step on the way. We know God is with us, so we step out in faith and do what we know to be right, trusting he will help us when we need him. The old principle of conduct is to avoid what is wrong, and to do what is right and good. No one can argue with this, but life in the Spirit introduces a new principle of conduct. Our actions now proceed from the life of the Spirit in us, which will guide us in natural and supernatural ways:

- **We now have the Spirit to guide us, not just the principles of good conduct**
- **The presence of God's Spirit will make a difference to what we do**
- **The Spirit knows the mind and will of God, and he will reveal it to us**

What will happen as we walk in the Spirit?

It may not be dramatic or sudden, but inevitably the life of the Holy Spirit within us will become evident, and things will begin to happen that did not happen before. One clear sign of this will be the growth of the fruit of the Spirit in us.

But life in the Spirit is not something we achieve as soon as we are baptised in the Holy Spirit. The process of inner transformation is part of walking in the Spirit - sometimes change will come quickly and easily, but at other times it will be slow and painful. This is all part of walking the walk. After Baptism in the Spirit there may be a wilderness experience, and we should not be discouraged by this – Jesus himself was taken into the wilderness to be tempted by the devil *Luke 4: 1-13*.

At times of difficulty and discouragement we need to:

- **Hold fast to what we believe**
- **Put our trust in God's promise – *"I am with you always"* Matthew. 28:20**
- **Seek fellowship, prayer, and support from other Christians**
- **Resist the lies and temptations of the devil**

We will come through our times of trial and be strengthened by them. Paul has a very positive view of this:

"And we know that in all things God works for the good of those who love him, who have been called according to his purposes" Romans 8:28.

In *Galatians 5: 16-18* he also reminds us:

"So I say, live by the Spirit, and you will not gratify the desires of the sinful nature. For the sinful nature desires what is contrary

to the Spirit, and the Spirit what is contrary to the sinful nature. They are in conflict with each other, so that you do not do what you want. But if you are led by the Spirit, you are not under law".

Living according to our own self-interest will direct us away from God and towards sin. We cannot live for God and ourselves at the same time – the two things are opposed to each other. So in order to yield to the Holy Spirit, we must resist the sinful nature, because as long as we want to maintain ourselves there will be little room for God. We must die to ourselves so that God can fill us more and more.

The desires of the sinful nature, sometimes called 'the flesh', are against the Spirit, and these desires are of the mind as well as of the body. As Paul puts it in *Ephesians 2:3 : "...gratifying the cravings of our sinful nature, and following its desires and thoughts".*

WHAT ARE THE DANGERS WE MUST GUARD AGAINST?

Pride and Self are the two most dangerous temptations we face.

Everything we do is for **his** glory, not for our glory. It can be hard to accept this, and to give him the credit, particularly when we have natural ability and are tempted to bask in the glory of things we achieve through our own strengths. But this is simply a question of **pride**, and *Proverbs 16:18* reminds us *"Pride goes before destruction, a haughty spirit before a fall".*

Baptism in the Holy Spirit is not a sign of superiority – if anything it underlines our weakness. It is because we are weak that we seek God's strength, and when God blesses us we do not ourselves get any stronger; it is simply that God's strength is now able to flow more freely through us. But the danger of human pride will be lurking in the shadows of our walk in the Spirit. God makes men and women strong in the power of his Spirit; they prosper, but instead of constantly acknowledging their natural weakness and humbling themselves before God, they can become proud, arrogant, and finally presumptuous in his presence. They think themselves without error, above correction – then comes the fall, and exclusion from God's blessing. Paul is an outstanding example of a man who knew his own weaknesses and relied on God's strength: *"For when I am weak, then I am strong" 2 Corinthians 12:10.* He thanked God for his weakness – look at what he achieved.

When we are baptised in the Holy Spirit we are just beginning. As we walk in the Spirit we will make many mistakes, we will have failures as well as successes. We must never let the successes make us proud, we must not talk too much about them, and we must give all the glory to God. Similarly, we should never allow our failures to lead us into despair. These too are stepping stones along the way, not stumbling blocks, and if we are humble we will learn from our mistakes. The proud never admit mistakes, so can never learn from them. If we are to be of any use to God we must admit our failures, learn from others, and accept their correction. Above all we need to remember the words of Jesus: *"apart from me you can do nothing" John 15:5.*

If our ego is not dealt with, our service will be spoiled.

Our natural reason and emotions can easily be mixed up with the impulses of the Spirit, especially when we have some knowledge of the matter concerned, or are personally involved. It is only humility that will safeguard us from speaking words as inspirations of the Spirit when the source is really our own reason and emotions. Baptism in the Holy Spirit is no short-cut to Christian maturity – indeed it often signals the breaking out of fresh conflicts which show us what we are really like. If the Holy Spirit is to be in full control, these conflicts must be resolved, self must be set aside, and all the glory must go to God. When the Spirit is in full control we will want to keep out of the limelight and give the glory to God, but sadly it's easy to remain self-centred, out for personal glory, looking for experiences rather than service, and for personal enjoyment more than for self-denial. All this is possible, but only for a limited time; the power will soon be withdrawn and only human strength will remain. The language may still be used, but the reality will no longer be there.

We must be honest and admit we have failed, and allow the Holy Spirit to search us and untangle us. The answer is in humble repentance before God, and before others if necessary. When we slip back into the old ways, it does not mean that the Holy Spirit has left us and the new life is over – it simply means that there is more work still to be done in us. The fact that the Holy Spirit has started work in us is the guarantee of the completion *Ephesians 1:14* because when the Spirit comes:

- **He inspires prayer; this will maintain our spiritual power,** *Romans 8:26.*

- He brings freedom in praise and worship; this maintains our relationship with God, *Acts 16:25.*
- He gives some a desire for intercession; this supports others, *1 Timothy.2:1.*
- He brings power to witness and evangelise; this draws others to Christ, *Acts 1:8.*
- He brings power for healing and deliverance; this produces wholeness and freedom, *Luke 9:1-2.*
- He nourishes social concern; this helps us not to become self-centred, *Acts 2:44-45.*
- He gives access to his gifts and ministries; this builds up the body of Christ, *1 Corinthians 12:4-31.*
- But most of all, he brings a new freedom, *Galatians.5:1.*

A fervent prayer

In the Pentecost meeting with the new Movements and Ecclesial Communities in St. Peter's Square, on May 30th 1998, to which I referred earlier and at which I was present, invited to respond on behalf of all those gathered to the words of **Pope John Paul II,** he also said:

"Today, to all of you gathered here in St. Peter's Square and to all Christians, I want to cry out: Be open and docile to the gifts of the Spirit! Accept with gratitude and obedience the charisms that the Spirit never ceases to bestow! Do not forget that each charism is given for the common good, that is, for the benefit of the whole Church!.. Today from this Cenacle of St. Peter's Square we raise up a fervent prayer. Come Holy Spirit, come and renew the face of the earth! Come with your seven gifts! Come Spirit of life, Spirit of truth, Spirit of communion and love! The Church and the world need you. Come Holy Spirit and make the charisms you have bestowed ever more fruitful. Give new strength and missionary zeal to these sons and daughters of yours who are gathered here. Enlarge their hearts, enliven their Christian commitment in the world. Make them courageous messengers of the Gospel, witnesses of the risen Jesus Christ, Redeemer and Saviour of mankind."

There must be a passion for freedom in our hearts, and an openness to receive from the Holy Spirit. If we are to be courageous messengers of the Gospel and witnesses of Jesus, we must be determined to hear the voice of the Spirit and to follow him - even when it means breaking established patterns and habits.

The Church needs all of us to use our gifts to play a fully active part in her life and mission. Pope John Paul II explained this on April 30th 1998 in these words:

"The Spirit is like a wind filling the sails of the great ship of the Church. If, however, we look at her closely, she uses numerous other small sails that are the hearts of the baptised. Everyone, dear friends, is invited to hoist their sails, to unfurl them with courage, and to permit the Spirit to act with all his sanctifying power. By allowing the Spirit to act in one's own life, one also makes the best contribution to the mission of the Church. Do not be afraid to unfurl your sails to the breath of the Spirit!"

Symbols of the Holy Spirit

In our first chapter we saw that, at first sight, some of the words used to describe the Holy Spirit can be difficult, but as we come to the end of our journey **towards a fuller life in the Holy Spirit**, let's look again at some of those words and remind ourselves of the richness of their meanings when used to describe the Spirit of God.

Wind   dramatic and powerful, gentle and caressing.

Fire   consuming and destroying, but energy and heat-producing.

Cloud   moving or static, over-shadowing, concealing, holding the promise of rain

Water   cleansing, life-giving, refreshing.

Oil   heat and light-producing, healing, a sign of consecration, a link to the sacraments.

Breath   essential for life, creative.

Light   a sign of the presence of God, helping us 'see' spiritually.

A Dove   symbol of peace and love, freedom and flight.

We need to become familiar with every attribute of the Holy Spirit – his power, his love, his creativity, his energy, and above all, his freedom. He will light a fire of love within us that will burn away our inhibitions and enable us to be salt and light for our world. We will commit ourselves to a new obedience and discover a new desire to serve with power. It is not enough to know him – we must let ourselves be empowered and led by the Spirit.

This brings us to our final question -

HOW DO WE STAY WITH THE SPIRIT, AND NOT SLIP BACK INTO THE OLD WAYS?

It's quite possible to fall out of the principle of grace and to bring ourselves under the law again. We saw earlier how angry Paul was when he saw the Galatian Christians allowing this to happen *Galatians chapter 3*. They wanted to have Christ, but also the Old Testament law, so that having started with the Spirit they were trying to reach the finish by their own natural energy and strength. In *Romans chapter 7*, Paul tells us that when he starts thinking about the law and trying to keep it, he is distracted from Christ and his provision of new life in the Holy Spirit, and so falls back into the old impotence and frustration. Only when he concentrates again on Christ, and takes himself back into walking in the Spirit, is he able to serve again with power:

"By dying to what once bound us, we have been released from the law so that we serve in the new way of the Spirit, and not in the old way of the written code" Romans 7: 6.

Some who start their new lives in the Spirit rejoicing in the free provision of God's grace, go on to try to reform themselves and society by the natural energy of their own constitutions, and run into frustration and failure. To be baptised in the Holy Spirit is to realise afresh that in everything we are to live, not out of ourselves and our own efforts, but out of God's provision of life and power in Christ. We are called to be salt and light: *"You are the salt of the earth. But if the salt loses its saltiness, how can it be made salty again? It is no longer good for anything, except to be thrown out and trampled by men. You are the light of the world... let your light shine before men, that they may see your good deeds and praise your Father in heaven" Matthew 5:13-16.* If we are to remain salty and light-giving we need the power of the Spirit in our lives.

To be filled with the Holy Spirit is to turn:

- **from law to Spirit**
- **from works to faith**
- **from self to God.**

But we must be careful not to subject ourselves to new legal systems of one kind or another, where we are bound to rigorous disciplines and to men's ideas.

We must keep ourselves in the freedom of the Spirit. **"Rigorous morality and strict law is the refuge of disappointed enthusiasts"** said an Anglican priest, **Rev. Tom Smail**, perhaps thinking of Paul's words in *Galatians 5:1: "It is for freedom that Christ has set us free. Stand firm, then, and do not let yourselves be burdened again by a yoke of slavery."*

To walk in the Spirit is:

- **to walk in the love, the freedom, and the power of God**
- **to listen to the voice and guidance of the Holy Spirit**
- **to do everything in his strength, not our own**

- **to do it all for the glory of Jesus and our Father.**

When we walk in the will of God we will have peace, and we will know when we divert from his path. Christ died to give us freedom; let's accept it now, and walk with him in the power and freedom of his Spirit. Then we'll begin to experience

A Fuller Life in the Holy Spirit

Discuss these statements with reference to the Scriptures:

Through the work of Jesus it is now possible for us to live a new life in the Spirit, but it isn't automatic

As we walk in this new life in the Spirit there are dangers, especially pride and self-interest, that will hinder us

It's important to stay with the Spirit, and avoid the temptation to return to the old ways

The Scriptures:

Matthew 5: 1-16 and Acts 2: 42-47

The Questions:

How would you describe walking in the Spirit?

What steps will you now take to help you live A Fuller Life in the Holy Spirit?

EPILOGUE

THE CENTURY OF THE HOLY SPIRIT

The twentieth century is often referred to as the Century of the Holy Spirit. From the beginning it was characterised by a series of amazing outpourings of the Spirit which occurred in different places from 1900 onwards. As the century began, on January 1st 1901, Pope Leo XIII prayed that the Holy Spirit would come again in power to the whole Church, and he sang the **Veni, Creator Spiritus!** (Come, Creator Spirit!) in his private chapel. Perhaps to his surprise, the first sign of an answer to his prayer was an experience of the presence and power of the Spirit at that moment in Topeka, Kansas, at the Bethel Bible School. This was followed in 1906 by revival at Number 312, Azusa Street, Los Angeles, California, a poor, run-down mission church pastored by William J. Seymour. Revival had also broken out in Wales in 1904-05 under Evan Roberts, a 26 year old lay minister in the Free Church chapels of the coal-mining valleys. These events heralded the arrival of the Pentecostal and Charismatic movements, which within a few years would be found all over the world.

As the century unfolded, a variety of traditional Protestant churches - Anglican, Episcopalian, Lutheran, Reformed, Methodist and Baptist - also experienced renewal in the power of the Spirit, and from the 1950s onwards the independent New Church or

House Church movement appeared in the United Kingdom and North America, quickly becoming established and spreading rapidly. Typical of these would be Pioneer, New Frontiers, and later the Vineyards. Only the Catholic and Orthodox Churches seemed unaffected by this new outpouring of the Spirit, until in 1967 a group of American Catholic students from Duquesne University were attending a weekend retreat, at which they too experienced an amazing outpouring of the Holy Spirit as they studied the early chapters of the Book of Acts. Signs of the Holy Spirit at work followed in some Orthodox Churches, and Messianic Judaism was born to complete the picture. The common factor shared by the Pentecostals, the Charismatics in the mainline denominations, the New or House Churches, and some other Charismatic Non-Denominational churches was Baptism in the Holy Spirit and the re-emergence of the charismata, the gifts of the Holy Spirit.

The above special outpourings of the Holy Spirit had a number of things in common:

- All were grass-roots events.
- All were characterised by great love, joy, and missionary zeal.
- All experienced artistic creativity, new music, song writing, and worship.
- There was a greater awareness and interest in the Second Coming of Christ.
- The charisms, supernatural gifts of the Holy Spirit, were freely poured out.
- There was a new appreciation of a shared experience leading to a growing ecumenism.
- Most had to face negativity, criticism, and even rejection by

other churches, and in the cases of some of the denominational churches negativity from their hierarchies and many members.
• Their experience was everywhere described as Baptism in the Spirit.

A personal view of the changes that followed

So what effect did all this have on the worldwide church in all its different expressions, and what changes in attitudes and practices resulted? Not surprisingly, these shared experiences gave rise to a much greater openness to Christians from other denominations, churches and fellowships. In the early days especially, the grace and power of the Spirit were often mediated to us through Christians outside our own circles, and this made us more aware of how much we had in common and how we needed each other. God seemed less concerned about our divisions than we were, and we read with new eyes *John 17:20-23* where Jesus prayed for unity for all his followers. We really understood from *Ephesians 4:3* that there IS a fundamental unity we are all called to keep. We ARE brothers and sisters in Christ because we all declare him our Saviour and Lord and share in a common baptism.

Since the Second Vatican Council in the 1960s, the Catholic Church has been 'irrevocably committed' to the ecumenical journey, and Popes Paul VI, John Paul II and Benedict XVI have all emphasised the important contribution to be made by those who have experienced a new outpouring of the Spirit in their lives. We have a special calling to establish closer relationships and friendships with those from other Christian expressions and traditions, but if we are to do this effectively we must first be sure of our own identity. For true and valid ecumenism to exist, those involved must be faithful to who they are and must accept others as they are

- it cannot be a matter of the lowest common denominator. That is not authentic ecumenism.

In Pope John Paul II's Encyclical Letter **'Ut Unum Sint'** (That They May Be One) published in 1995, he again encouraged all Catholics to see other Christians as brothers and sisters in Christ; to meet and pray with them; to dialogue and share with them; to learn about them and from them; to do together whatever can be done in good conscience; and to give public witness to our shared faith alongside them. He fully acknowledged that this would not be easy, and that many Catholics would be challenged by it. But he asked us to look deeply into our hearts and to acknowledge our weaknesses and past failings before the Lord, fully recognising that whilst we must all play our parts, full unity is something only the Holy Spirit can bring about. We must work for it, pray for it, and allow the Spirit to make it happen. We are, after all, those who know the power of the Spirit.

The powerful outpourings of the Holy Spirit, experienced by so many different parts of the body of Christ in the twentieth century in particular, have shown us just how much the worldwide Christian family needs the love, grace and power of the Spirit of God to bring us new life and to equip us for all that lies ahead. The Spirit helps us grow in love - for God, for ourselves, and for one another - and he gives us both the desire and the power to evangelise. To do that effectively there needs to be a basic unity among us *"so that the world may believe that you have sent me" John 17:21*. So let's now look briefly at the Catholic Charismatic Renewal, a very important part of this mighty move of God's Holy Spirit.

THE CATHOLIC CHARISMATIC RENEWAL

Many people have heard something about the Catholic Charismatic Renewal (CCR), and without really understanding what it is may well have decided it's not for them. That's a great pity – it's a gift from God and has something very important to contribute to the life of the Church, as we have already seen. So against this background, I will try to summarise in a short and easy to understand way what lies at the heart of the Catholic Charismatic Renewal, and why it is important to the Church. I'll begin by looking at the two key words 'charismatic' and 'renewal' as used in this context.

A charism is a special gift of the Holy Spirit. Its root is in the Greek word 'charis' meaning 'grace'. Every charism is a special gift of grace because it is supernaturally given by the Holy Spirit to equip the recipient to undertake particular tasks or services for the benefit of the Church. So the word **'charismatic'** is here used to describe something which has its origins **in**, is inspired **by**, and contains the power **of** the Holy Spirit.

The Oxford English Dictionary defines **'renewal'** in these words: **"among charismatic Christians, the state or process of being renewed in the Holy Spirit".**

So renewal is a process, usually beginning when the Holy Spirit responds to someone's request to renew their spiritual life. Every Christian needs on-going spiritual renewal, and here we are clearly reminded that this is an activity of the Holy Spirit.

Drawing all this together, we can say that the Catholic Charismatic Renewal is in essence both the action and the result of an outpouring of the Holy Spirit, which brings a new or renewed experience of God's life and power into the lives of his people. It is a sovereign work of the Holy Spirit of God because it is not something we own or control. Through it we are invited to hand our lives over to God, to give the control back to him. We allow God to **be** God and to work in us through his Holy Spirit to equip and empower us to live effective Christian lives. This renewal is freely offered to anyone who asks – we just need to be willing to invite the Holy Spirit to release his power in us and to bring alive the graces of our Baptism. But the Spirit not only brings alive all that we have already received through the sacraments of our Christian initiation, he also comes again in power to equip us with new gifts for service and mission.

THE BEGINNINGS

At the beginning of the 1960s, Pope John XXIII called a major international council of the Catholic Church, called The Second Vatican Council. A key part of his motivation in calling the Council was a desire to see the Holy Spirit bring new vision and power into the life of the worldwide Church. So he invited every Catholic to join him in praying for an opening of the windows of the Church to the wind of the Spirit – for a new Pentecost in our time. God answered the prayers of his people, and among the many fruits of the Council was a much greater appreciation of the gifts of the Holy Spirit in the life of the Church, and a blossoming of new ecclesial movements and communities.

Among these we find the Catholic Charismatic Renewal, which began in February 1967 among a group of about 25 American students from Duquesne University, who attended a weekend retreat at which they experienced an amazing outpouring of the Holy Spirit. Two of their leaders had already seen their own spiritual lives transformed through the power of the Holy Spirit at a Protestant prayer meeting when hands were laid on them, and this had caused in them a new spiritual hunger and thirst. As they and the students read from the first four chapters of the Book of Acts, the question they were asking was why did their own experience of God lack the power and effects they were reading about among the first disciples of Jesus? As they then prayed in the chapel at the retreat house for a renewal of their Confirmation grace, they experienced a sovereign move of the Holy Spirit as God revealed to them his majesty, his glory, and his merciful love, in a powerful upper room experience. This was the experience we usually call Baptism in the Holy Spirit.

From these simple beginnings, Baptism in the Holy Spirit spread rapidly through the campuses of the Catholic Universities in the USA, and into the wider Church. No grass-roots spiritual movement has ever spread as far or as fast as the CCR, and ten years later more than 100 million Catholics in over 100 countries could testify to similar experiences. Today there are charismatic Catholics in more than 200 countries.

In a letter to Patti Gallagher Mansfield, one of the Duquesne weekend retreatants, in February 1991, Dr. Vinson Synan, a Pentecostal Church historian, wrote: **"One never knows the effect of any one meeting when the Spirit of God moves. I believe** the Duquesne Weekend will have to go down in history as one of the most important prayer meetings that ever occurred, especially in modern times."

THE CHURCH HIERARCHY

From the very beginning, following a time of careful discernment and theological and pastoral reflection, the Church has welcomed the Catholic Charismatic Renewal. Pope Paul VI received the early leaders in Rome in 1973 and again in1975, when he described the CCR as **"a chance for the Church and the world"**. On numerous public occasions, Pope John Paul II expressed his personal support. For example: **"Because of the Spirit, the church preserves a continual youthful vitality. And the Charismatic Renewal is an eloquent manifestation of this vitality today, a bold statement of *'what the Spirit is saying to the Churches' Revelation 2:7!'*** Similarly Pope Benedict XVI has been unfailing in his commitment and encouragement both before and since his election as Supreme Pontiff.

In 1993, during my first term as President, the International Council of the Catholic Charismatic Renewal was given official recognition and granted formal Church Statutes as a body to promote the CCR throughout the Church. So the Catholic Charismatic Renewal is not some strange, fringe organisation, but an accepted, approved, and encouraged current of fruitful life at the very heart of the Catholic Church, bringing new life and spiritual power to millions of ordinary men and women.

WHAT FORM DOES THE CATHOLIC CHARISMATIC RENEWAL TAKE?

The CCR is not a single unified worldwide movement, and it does not have a human founder or formal programme of initiation and membership lists as other movements do. Neither is it a special devotion to the Holy Spirit, a strange new spirituality for some particular people, or just a network of prayer groups and communities. In 1990 in **'Spiritual Journey'** Cardinal Suenens explained it in these words: **"To interpret the Renewal as a movement among other movements is to misunderstand its nature: it is a movement of the Spirit offered to the entire Church, and destined to rejuvenate every facet of the Church's life. The soul of Renewal, Baptism in the Spirit, is a grace of Pentecostal refreshment offered to all Christians."** The CCR is a highly diverse collection of individuals, groups, communities, ministries and activities, usually quite independent of one another, in different stages and modes of development and with different emphases. One of the special characteristics of the CCR is the enormous variety of its expressions and ministries, all inspired by the Holy Spirit and carried out in his power, which have a home under the CCR umbrella. Everyone shares the same foundational experience of the empowering presence of the Holy Spirit through Baptism in the Spirit, but the emphasis is on relationships and networks rather than on structures and organisation.

These patterns of informal relationships are to be found at local, diocesan, national and international levels, and are characterised by free association, dialogue and collaboration. Many groups feel they are part of a big charismatic family – by their very nature they are related to each other and they do not see any need to be formally integrated into an ordered charismatic structure locally or nationally. They know they are already fully part of the Church under the hierarchy, and that's what is important. The CCR does not exist to build up a big organisation – the simple desire of those involved is that as many others as possible should also have their Christian lives renewed by the Holy Spirit. Some organisation may be necessary to facilitate this, but it should be kept to a minimum. In a General Audience on October 12th 1966, Pope Paul VI reminded us: **"If we really love the Church, the main things we must do is to foster in it an outpouring of the Divine Paraclete, the Holy Spirit."**

So with these words in mind, in the Charismatic Renewal there are the following simple structures:

• Diocesan Service Committees (DSCs) which relate to the local bishop and serve the CCR groups in the diocese.

• National Service Committees (NSCs) which perform the same function at national level and relate to their national Conferences of Bishops.

• International Catholic Charismatic Renewal Services (ICCRS), which has its office in Vatican premises in Rome, relating to the Church primarily through the Pontifical Council for Laity, communicating and serving the worldwide CCR, and building relationships with the other ecclesial movements in the Church whilst maintaining a particular openness to other expressions and parts of the body of Christ outside the Catholic Church.

• The Catholic Fraternity of Covenant Communities, serving
the large number of new charismatic communities worldwide
which have sprung up as another fruit of the CCR.

I believe it's important to remember that: **"Baptism in the Spirit is
captive to no camp, whether liberal or conservative. Nor is it
identified with any one movement, nor with one style of prayer,
worship, or community. On the contrary, we believe that the gift
of Baptism in the Holy Spirit belongs to the Christian inheritance
of all those sacramentally initiated into the Church."** These
words, taken from **'Fanning the Flame'** by McDonnell and
Montague, The Liturgical Press, Minnesota 1991, help to explain
why the Catholic Charismatic Renewal has not attempted to build
up a big organisation and structure, but simply wants to release the
grace of Baptism in the Spirit in the lives of all Christians.

Although the CCR differs from other new movements as outlined
above, it is generally spoken of by the Church as a movement, and
therefore very much included in the statements about the
movements made over recent years by the Popes and a number of
Bishops' Conferences. For example, in his document on the state of
the Catholic Church in Europe, **'Ecclesia in Europa'**, we find the
following comments by **Pope John Paul II** in section 15:

**"The Gospel continues to bear fruit in lay associations, in groups
devoted to prayer and the apostolate, as well as through the
presence and growth of new movements and ecclesial realities.
In each of them the one Spirit finds ways of awakening renewed
dedication to the Gospel, generous openness to the service of
others, and a Christian life marked by Gospel radicalism and**

missionary zeal".
These words are certainly true of the Catholic Charismatic Renewal, a current of grace in the great river of the Church, bringing the power of Pentecost into every part of her life and mission and offering **A Fuller Life in the Holy Spirit** to everyone.

Charles Whitehead

Further copies of this book
can be obtained from

Goodnews Books
Upper level
St. John's Church Complex
296 Sundon Park Road
Luton, Beds. LU3 3AL

www.goodnewsbooks.net
orders@goodnewsbooks.net
01582 571011